The Rivers and Ravines

A Play

by Heather McDonald

A SAMUEL FRENCH ACTING EDITION

SAMUEL FRENCH

FOUNDED 1830

New York Hollywood London Toronto

SAMUELFRENCH.COM

IMPORTANT BILLING AND CREDIT REQUIREMENTS

All producers of THE RIVERS AND RAVINES *must* give credit to the Author of the Play in all programs distributed in connection with performances of the Play and in all instances in which the title of the Play appears for purposes of advertising, publicizing or otherwise exploiting the Play and/or a production. The name of the Author *must* also appear on a separate line, in which no other name appears, immediately following the title, and *must* appear in size of type not less than fifty percent the size of the title type.

CAUTIONARY NOTE

The text of this play makes reference to several songs or pieces of music still under copyright protection. Producers are hereby cautioned that rights to produce THE RIVERS AND RAVINES do not include permission to use any of this music. Such permission must be procured from the owners of the copyrights to the various pieces of music, who may be contacted c/o A.S.C.A.P.; 1 Lincoln Plaza; New York, NY 10023. Or, c/o B.M.I.; 320 W. 57th St.; New York, NY 10019.

A DEDICATION

I could not have written the play this way without him,
and so, I dedicate "The Rivers and Ravines" to Bennett
Minton because he is so much a part of it.

Gemeinschaft — term to describe the associated values and feelings of people whose primary allegiance is to the group or community.

Gesellschaft — term to describe the compartmentalized, specialized, utilitarian relationships that typify urban life.

It takes the greatest courage
To go on
Acting to the end
As do the rivers and ravines.
　　　　　—Boris Pasternak

THE RIVERS AND RAVINES premiered on February 26, 1988 at Arena Stage in Washington, DC; Zelda Fichandler, Producing Director; William Stewart, Managing Director; and Douglas C. Wager, Associate Producing Director; under the direction of Douglas C. Wager and Paul Walker, with setting by David M. Glenn, costumes by Marjorie Slaiman, lighting by Nancy Schertler, sound by Eric Annis, vocal consultation by Nadia Venesse, production coordination by Guy Bergquist, stage management by Jessica Evans, and with the following cast:

Ethelyn MacCormick . . . . Tana Hicken

Ray MacCormick, Ensemble . . . . Henry Strozier

Winona Tarlow . . . . Gale Garnett

John Harper . . . . John Leonard

Tess Harper . . . . Lili Flanders

Carl Pritchard, Ensemble . . . . Walt MacPherson

Molly Pritchard, Reporter . . . . Marissa Copeland

Bill Hoddupp . . . . Stanley Anderson

Caleb Stratman, Ensemble . . . . Terrence Currier

Wordsworth (Wordy) Stratman, Ensemble . . . . Bob Kirsh

CAST CONTINUED

Maudaline Stratman, Ginny. . . . . Cary Anne Spear

Emil the Fifth. . . . . Richard Bauer

Alice Darke . . . . Halo Wines

Ted, Cameraman, Auctioneer, Ensemble. . . David Marks

TV Director, Ensemble . . . . Paul Walker

SETTING

A rural community in eastern Colorado. The set should be spare and abstract, suggesting place rather than realistically portraying the various scene settings. It should create an overall environment within which the play can unfold with ease. In the original production, the two significant "set" pieces were a large, weathered, slatted barn wall with two doors in it and a stage covered with dirt. Throughout the play, place is suggested by the use of a few pieces and props, and, most especially, lighting.

CHARACTERS

PRINCIPALS

Ethelyn MacCormick — early 50s. farmwife

Ray MacCormick — early 50s, farmer

Winona Tarlow — early 40s, part Hopi Indian, owner of Winona Tarlow's Cafe & Bar

John Harper — late 30s, rancher, later property management consultant

Tess Harper — mid 30s, farmwife

Carl Pritchard — mid 40s, banker

Molly Pritchard — his daughter, 14, runs off to Clown College in Sarasota, Florida

Bill Hoddupp — early 40s, minister, later founder of Rural Crisis Hotline

Caleb Stratman — rancher, mid 50s

Wordsworth (Wordy) Stratman — his son, 15

Maudaline Stratman — his daughter, 8

Emil the Fifth *(pronounced Amyl)* — mid 50s, farmer

Alice Darke — late 30s, Farmers Home Administration loan officer, later works as volunteer on Rural Crisis Hotline

BIT PARTS

Ted and Ginny — 2 USDA representatives

T. Bart Heyho — TV gameshow host

Reporter

Cameraman

News director

Auctioneer

THE RIVERS AND RAVINES

ACT I
SCENE 1

SCENE: The editing room of a TV station. A REPORTER, NEWS DIRECTOR and CAMERAMAN are editing "clips" on a "TV monitor" assembling a news report. They're eating hamburgers, chips, sandwiches, Twinkies, drinking coffee and smoking cigarettes. This scene should be done live with the TV people down center and the actors coming into light behind them when their "clip" comes up. The feeling of assembling a newstory should be suggested rather than done realistically on tape.

REPORTER. Damn, I said no mayonnaise.

DIRECTOR. Okay, let's see what you've got.

REPORTER. The first clip is the the town with boarded-up shops.

CAMERAMAN. That's the main drag.

REPORTER. Maybe I could add a voice-over about how many stores closed in the past year.

DIRECTOR. Maybe you could do your intro over it.

CAMERAMAN. We've got that live in the church.

REPORTER. Do you have mayonnaise, too?

CAMERAMAN. Yeah.

DIRECTOR. Any other beauty shots?

11

REPORTER. Lonely farmhouses stark against the evening sky, a rusted combine in a field, that sort of thing.

CAMERAMAN. That's the church where the funeral was held.

DIRECTOR. We'll use that. I think we'll just focus on the funeral.

REPORTER. That's inside the church.

CAMERAMAN. I didn't get any ketchup for my fries. You have any extra?

REPORTER. Uh uh.

CAMERAMAN. Shit.

DIRECTOR. Who's this?

REPORTER. The minister. Bill Hoddupp. *(beat)* That's the husband. John Harper.

DIRECTOR. Is he crying?

REPORTER. Yes.

DIRECTOR. You have that in close-up?

CAMERAMAN. A little further on.

DIRECTOR. Great. That'll look great. Can you freeze on that ... the tear.

REPORTER. He found her, you know.

DIRECTOR. Jesus, it really is a nice little story.

REPORTER. I'm telling you, I need more time to do this story justice.

DIRECTOR. Three minutes, that's it.

REPORTER. Oh, come on.

CAMERAMAN. Are you going to eat that?

DIRECTOR. It's just the suicide and the funeral.

REPORTER. No, it's a bigger story than that. I've got a lot of good stuff.

DIRECTOR. But it's not news. People are tired of it.

They've heard it before.

REPORTER. But it's still a story.

DIRECTOR. The news angle is the suicide. It's a terrific suicide. You get three minutes.

CAMERAMAN. Are you going to eat that?

REPORTER. Just because I eat slowly and chew my food and don't wolf it down like a pig doesn't mean I'm finished yet.

CAMERAMAN. This guy calls himself Emil the Fifth.

DIRECTOR. Great name.

EMIL. Yes, I think the problem is getting much worse much faster, and I think it's going to get a lot worse until our government gets rid of the cheap food policy and the so-called surplus that they have in storage because as long as we have it, every time any commodity gets to where it would make a dollar, the government dumps another bunch of that surplus on the market.

DIRECTOR. No, we don't need this. Go on.

CALEB. Of course, you have your loudmouths. The best way to find out what's going on is to listen to the farmers who aren't saying anything.

RAY. Mi puo riprare questo orologia?

REPORTER. I don't know what's with this guy.

ETHELYN. I've always thought Italian was such a happy language.

CAMERAMAN. He was weird.

CALEB. A sheep knows that every time it bleats it loses a mouthful.

CARL. My daughter, Molly, ran away. She's 14. Here's a picture. Maybe you could do something.

(WORDY unfolds a piece of paper.)

DIRECTOR. Who's this?

CAMERAMAN. Some kid.

REPORTER. Wordsworth Stratman. His family's just been foreclosed on.

WORDY. I'd like to read something. It's from the creed of the Future Farmers of America. "I believe in the future of farming with a faith born not of words but of deeds and achievements won by the present and past generations of agriculturists in the promise of better days through better ways even as the better things we now enjoy have come to us from struggles of former years."

DIRECTOR. No, no, go on. *(CAMERAMAN stuffs a Twinkie in his mouth.)*

REPORTER. *(to CAMERAMAN:)* Do you really have to eat that shit? You are making me sick.

DIRECTOR. Who's the little girl?

CAMERAMAN. She's the Future Farmer's sister.

MAUDALINE. My name is Maudaline Stratman. I'm eight years old. My mommy said, she didn't work hard all her life to live in a trailer park. My dad said, it's a mobile home. I asked her why she was going away. She said, Maudaline, we are going to the poorhouse. I asked her where the poorhouse was. I asked my dad if we could get ice cream and he told me to shut up.

DIRECTOR. Hmm, I kind of like that.

REPORTER. The guy complaining about the loud-mouths. He's her father. Caleb Stratman. And the Future

Farmer is her brother.

(An uncomfortable looking ETHELYN.)

ETHELYN. They are my friends. Please. It's awful close to home.

CAMERAMAN. That's all we got on her. She wasn't too cooperative.

RAY. Mi dis piace, non capisco.

DIRECTOR. There's that Italian guy again.

REPORTER. Here's the husband again.

JOHN. When she died at 5:13 in the morning, she looked happy. She got this big smile and her hands just opened at her sides. Ethelyn was there, too, she saw it. When someone dies, it's like you've been hit hard in the stomach. You lose your breath for a moment and everything stops. Then when it all comes back, you have an empty house.

DIRECTOR. What's that he's holding?

REPORTER. It's his wife's jewelry.

CAMERAMAN. Ooooh, heartbreaker, heartbreaker.

REPORTER. You can be such an asshole sometimes.

DIRECTOR. We can use both shots.

WINONA. Goddammit! Don't you understand? His wife is dead.

DIRECTOR. Who's this?

CAMERAMAN. Some Indian spook.

REPORTER. It gets better. We've got yelling.

WINONA. Something dreadful has happened here. A storm strikes and the next morning some man in a pressed safari suit and a brand new plaid shirt and skin that is too tanned for this time of year shows up wanting to know exactly what is was like, exactly how it feels to be showing the world today's pile of rubble instead of yesterday's handbuilt home.

DIRECTOR. I wonder if we can edit around this. I like the yelling.

WINONA. Get that thing out of my face. After you're done here, some editor will look through this film and confirm our existence by finding 34 seconds of drama to lead into the sports report.

DIRECTOR. So. We've got tears and yelling. *(beat)*

CAMERAMAN. Are we talking Emmys or what?

(BLACKOUT)

SCENE 2

SCENE: WINONA Down Center in SPOT. CAST stand in shadows on perimeter.

WINONA. My name is Winona Tarlow, owner of Winona Tarlow's Cafe and Bar. I've lived most all my life here. Grew up on a reservation not far from here. My mother was a full-blooded Hopi Indian. We lost our land, too, although that was some time back. Every year about this time I go with some other women to the Indian cliff dwellings at Mesa Verde to pray for balance. We have a butterfly event, a crazy dog event, a gift and a vision event. You don't believe me? It's true. Yesterday I saw a white cat somersault backwards down Crawson Street. You don't believe me. It's true. A white cat somersaulting backwards is always a sign of things being out of balance. This is a story about vision and balance, and these are the people in the story.

(LIGHTS up on characters as they are introduced.)

WINONA. Carl Pritchard runs the bank, and that's his daughter Molly, 14. John Harper over there, rancher. And his wife, Tess. Bill Hoddupp, he's pastor of the Full Gospel Lighthouse Church. Caleb Stratman, a cattleman, his daughter, Maudaline, 8, his son, Wordsworth, 15. That's Emil the Fifth and over there's Alice Darke. She's senior loan officer down at the Farmers Home Administration. Ray and Ethelyn MacCormick. They've just been named "Farm Family of the Year." Well, that's about it. We know what happens. All that is left is how it happens. Let's go back to where this story begins. We're in eastern Colorado. It's July the 4th, 1977. Independence Day. *(WINONA levitates ever so slightly. Somehow, a shift in spirit is achieved. This should be done with lights and music and is not an actual physical lifting of the actor.)* Go to a mountain top. Find a lonely place and rub a stone in a circle on a rock for hours and days on end and cry for a vision.

(A horseshoe flies in from off.)

SCENE 3

SCENE: LIGHTS slowly rise to reveal: 1977. A burst of FIREWORKS. A sumptuous Fourth of July barbeque. Fried chicken, baked beans, potato salad. A picnic table. Lots of red, white and blue. Traditional Fourth of July songs. Streamers, LAUGHTER, a feeling of euphoria.

A horseshoe flies in.

Overlapping dialogue.

CALEB. Wordy, careful with those horseshoes. Winona, you'd better move. He doesn't have such good aim.

WINONA. Thank you, Caleb.

CARL. I hear Floyd Burns has grown an inch since school let out.

ETHELYN. Ray, careful, no, you're backing in crooked ... to the right, no, you're about to hit — *(CRUNCH.)*

WINONA. There goes the extra chair.

TED. Remember to leave room for pie.

CARL. I'll check the coals.

EMIL. You want to put that beer in my cooler?

MOLLY. Kiss the corpse. Kiss the corpse.

WORDY. Leave me alone, Molly.

MOLLY. Pickle breath.

JOHN. *(observing GINNY putting on suntan lotion)* Are you from California?

GINNY. I freckle up real easy.

ALICE. Close the trunk.

CARL. Molly, you don't put jello on hotdogs.

TED. Wordy, how about a hamburger?

WORDY. I don't eat onions.

TED. I'll take them off.

WORDY. I don't eat anything onions have touched.

CALEB. If you don't start behaving, I'll take you home and you'll miss the fireworks.

GINNY. He can have mine. It doesn't have onions.

TESS. *(She is pregnant.)* Would you bring that ... yeah ... you know, next to the thing.

CALEB. What do you say?

WORDY. Thank you.

MOLLY. Kiss the corpse. Kiss the corpse.

WORDY. Bug off.

TESS. I love the Fourth of July.

CARL. You kids stop throwing those weenies around.

(A burst of FIREWORKS. "Ooooh, aaaahh." a SPOT captures RAY and ETHELYN. The barbecue freezes.)

RAY. Independence Day.

ETHELYN. We hold these truths to be self evident.

RAY. That all men are created equal—

ETHELYN. —and are endowed by their Creator—

RAY. —with certain inalienable rights.

ETHELYN. That if you have a dream.

RAY. I have a dream.

ETHELYN. And you work hard.

RAY. I work hard.

ETHELYN. I mean, really hard.

RAY. I work really hard.

ETHELYN. That you can get ahead.

RAY. That you can send your kids to college.

ETHELYN. That your children can have good teeth.

RAY. That you can be number one.

ETHELYN. But what if we all have dreams and work hard? How can we all be number one?

RAY. We can all be number one at different times.

(Flash of FIREWORKS. "Oooooooh, aaaahhh.")

ETHELYN. Aren't a lot more people going to be number 2 or 15 or 71 than number 1?

RAY. Ethelyn, it all works out. Take my word.

ETHELYN. What if something goes wrong? What if you never get to be number one?

WINONA. Go to a mountain top.

(Flash of FIREWORKS. The barbecue comes back to life.)

ETHELYN. I think I just saw a cow jump over the moon.

CARL. *(Taps a glass to get attention.)* Excuse me ... everyone ... excuse me, I'd like to make a toast.

EMIL. Oh, Carl, sit down, you're always making toasts.

CARL. I would like to make a toast to our friends, Ginny and Ted, from the United States Department of Agriculture.

("Hear, hear!")

Ray. Good ribs, Ted.

Ted. Thanks, but I have to give credit to Winona's special barbecue sauce.

Tess. Yeah, Winona.

Caleb. I propose a toast—

(A horseshoe flies wildly through the air.)

Caleb. Wordy, sit down. Sit on your hands. On your hands. *(beat)* I propose a toast to say thanks to Ted and Ginny for putting on this real fine Fourth of July barbecue and this spread for us.

(Claps, cheers.)

Ted. And I toast all of you. Ginny and I are glad to be here today. It's communities like this that are the backbone of America.

Ginny. I'd like to second that. I grew up in a community a lot like this, and I'm excited about being here today.

Ted. If everyone has gotten something to eat, I'd like to take a moment and talk to you about something. We're here to talk about the future and our roles in that future. Ginny wants to share with you a report put together back at the USDA in Washington. Ginny.

Ginny. Thank you, Ted. We've just completed a major government study of future economic trends called "Global 2000."

John. I'm listening, I'm just getting a little more.

Tess. Oh, please don't eat any more beans. *(Some laughs.)*

JOHN. Tess doesn't like me eating beans.

GINNY. This report paints a very bright picture for farmers in the future. The economists are telling us that
after decades of falling food prices, the price of food is
projected to increase 95% over the next decade.

(Some clapping and cheers.)

GINNY. We are the world's leaders in agriculture. I
know there's been a declining trend in the farm popu-
lation in recent years, but that declining trend is actually
a positive sign, a sign of a very strong agricultural
economy. We will need fewer farmers in the future, but
these few farmers must be better farmers and you could
be leading the way.

BILL. *(Sneezes loudly.)* Excuse me.

GINNY. You will have to operate on a faster track and
the race will go to the mighty and the swift.

JOHN. So what you're saying is that we've got to start
being more productive.

GINNY. I think so.

TED. We don't want to be going backwards, *(Hesitates
on JOHN'S name.)* John. We always want to be moving
forward. This report indicates that we will eventually be
unable to satisfy world hunger needs.

GINNY. So it's our duty to try and feed the world and to
plant fencepost to fencepost in that effort.

TED. Let's show the world that the heartland of
America is extending its heart to the whole world. Our
motto is: Don't be afraid to be big. Don't be afraid to
be big.

EMIL. I can't afford to get any bigger.

TED. Yes, you can. You can borrow.

TESS. But how will we pay it back?

TED. You don't ever have to pay it back.

CALEB. What?

GINNY. That's what "perpetual debt" is all about. We've been spending some time down at the bank with Carl and he's going to talk to you about some of the details like "perpetual debt."

EMIL. Here comes Carl and his charts.

CARL. I heard that, Emil. Now folks, it took me some time to get used to the idea of "perpetual debt." I thought it was a crazy idea at first, but I'm telling you it is the wave of the future. Because that land you are sitting on is going up and up in price and is worth more every day. So you might feel kind of funny about going into debt to buy new machinery, equipment or more land, but with "perpetual debt" you can pass that debt on to your children and to your children's children with no worries or fear, because the land, your collateral, is worth more even while you do nothing, even while you sleep.

EMIL. I don't like the idea of being in debt, of owing anybody.

CALEB. What if something goes wrong? What if those figures aren't correct?

TED. I understand your concerns, but you are sitting on a pile of gold and you've got to have the vision about what to do with that pile of gold.

JOHN. *(to group:)* I think I understand what they're saying. *(to TED and GINNY:)* You're talking about vision and risk.

TED. Yes.

EMIL. Something about this just doesn't sit right with me.

TED. Now, Emil, don't take this the wrong way, but I think you're going backwards. You need more land.

EMIL. I don't have the money to buy more land.

TED. That's why we're here.

ALICE. Farmer's Home can lend you the money.

EMIL. Alice ... maybe you're right. Maybe I am being too cautious.

RAY. I think we are being too cautious. I'd like to expand. I've got ambitions.

EMIL. I've got ambitions.

CALEB. We've all got ambitions, but you can't get something for nothing in this world. Just remember that.

ALICE. Maybe that's enough business for one day.

GINNY. I'll put another round of burgers on the grill.

TED. If any of you would like to talk further about all this, sign your name to this list and Alice can arrange an appointment for Monday.

ALICE. I'll leave it right here by Ethelyn's pie.

CARL. If you don't come to see me, I'll come to see you. *(People come forward and sign the piece of paper.)*

TED. How about you, don't you want to feed the world?

WINONA. I'm not a farmer. I'm Hopi Indian. I don't own land.

TED. Well then, get a loan and buy yourself some.

WINONA. Who would own it?

TED. Why, you would.

WINONA. Who will own all of their things, all the things they're putting up for collateral? Who will own their land? Sounds like you will, and that sounds like Communism to me.

TED. I'll tell you one thing for sure, when American goes Communist, we'll be the best damn Communists in the world.

CALEB. I think the kids got in the beer. Wordy just threw up. I'm taking him home.

TED. Did everyone get enough to eat? Hell, I'm still hungry. Come on, everybody, let's eat again. There are buckets of good food left. *(People eat.)*

BILL. I'd like to try some of Ethelyn's pie.

TED. *(to CARL.)* This is a grand day, isn't it? A grand day.

CARL. It sure is. *(Comes down to WINONA.)* Hey, Winona.

WINONA. Hey, Carl. *(CARL comes to stand beside WINONA. She's looking at the sky.)*

CARL. Always wanted to own a small country bank. The lack of bureaucracy. Doing things when I want the way I want. Being a part of a community. That's my dream, Winona. *(pause)* What are you looking at?

WINONA. When a mare's tails are seen in the sky, it is a sign of foul weather. If you see a naked child dancing, there will soon be a drought. *(Everyone begins moving slowly.)*

(Envelopes float down from above.)

MAUDALINE. *(Plays hopscotch.)*
Hey diddle diddle
The cat and the fiddle
The cow jumped over the moon
The little dog laughed
To see such sport
And the dish ran away with the spoon.

(A snowstorm of envelopes.)

(DIM OUT)

SCENE 4

SCENE: LIGHTS up. It is 1985. CARL, CALEB, ALICE, RAY, ETHELYN and EMIL open the envelopes. JOHN doesn't. A fugue.

CALEB. August 14, 1985.

RAY. United States Department of Agriculture. Farmers Home Administration.

JOHN. Form FmHA1924-25. U.S. Government Printing Office.

EMIL. Notice of Intent to Take Adverse Action.

CALEB. Dear Caleb Stratman,

RAY. As outlined below,

JOHN. your account with us is delinquent

EMIL. or there are other problems affecting your

borrowing relationship with us.

ETHELYN. Ray?

EMIL. Goddam sonuvabitch shit.

CALEB. You are behind schedule on your loan installments

RAY. which is a violation of your agreement.

JOHN. So when are you going to come take my land?

EMIL. If this violation is not corrected

CALEB. by one or more of the actions described in form 1924-26, we will need to accelerate your debts and

JOHN. eventually foreclose on your real estate and chattels.

ETHELYN. There's a small child dancing naked in the field.

RAY. If you wish to apply for a hearing,

ETHELYN. There's a small child dancing naked in the field.

RAY. complete part one of form 1924-27.

ETHELYN. It looks like Nathan.

RAY. You may appear in person with or without an attorney.

ETHELYN. I think of Nathan often these days, riding his Cherokee tractor up and down the driveway.

CALEB. Several methods of curing defaults or liquidation are available.

EMIL. If you prefer to use one of the methods listed in part 3,

JOHN. check the appropriate box,

CALEB. check the appropriate box,

RAY. check the apporporiate box.

EMIL. Goddamn sonuvabitch shit.

CALEB. Maudaline, come along.

JOHN. Tess? Tess?

CARL. *(CARL is seated at his desk reading a letter. TED stands near him reading the letter aloud.)* Dear Carl Pritchard,

TED. Our institution felt it was necessary to flag your bank loan with us as a problem loan and we'll be watching it more closely. You are going to have to do the same all the way down the line. In going over your books, we discovered many seriously delinquent loans. You've got to call in those farm loans. Sincerely.

CALEB. Maudaline, come along. Tell Wordy we're going in to town.

MAUDALINE. Can we get ice cream?

ALICE. *(Reads piece of paper she's holding.)* Notice of Intent to Take Adverse Action Against Farmers Home Administration Branch #32.

TED. Alice, I'm real sorry, but you've got to call in those loans.

(LIGHTS cross fade.)

SCENE 5

SCENE: ALICE DARKE is in her Farmers Home Administration office. RAY and ETHELYN are there holding many files.

THE DRAMA BOOK SHOP

250 West 40th St
New York, NY 10018
PHONE: (212) 944-0595
FAX: (212) 730-8739
TOLL FREE: 1-800-322-0595

1059996 Reg 2 ID 580 1:25 pm 12/08/17

S RIVERS & RAVINES	1 @	9.95	9.95
SUBTOTAL			9.95
SALES TAX - 8.875%			.88
TOTAL			10.83
CASH PAYMENT			11.00
CHANGE			.17

No exchanges or refunds. incl. scripts.
www.dramabookshop.com

RAY. My dad hung onto this land through *the Depression,* and now I'm losing it.

ALICE. I don't want you to go away thinking I think you're bad managers. We all got fooled. No one ever imagined that the farm economy would go this bad.

RAY. The only time I have to ask anyone for anything is when I have to come here and ask you for money. I don't like it.

ALICE. No one forced you. You signed on the dotted line. You were going to pay it back and if you can't ever pay it back, let's get out of it the best we can.

ETHELYN. Alice, I went to the Thomas Jefferson Junior High School prom with your brother. He gave me a wrist corsage.

ALICE. It's not right.

ETHELYN. We won first place in the dance contest.

ALICE. It's just not right. I know that.

ETHELYN. We danced the foxtrot.

ALICE. My advice to you is liquidate a major portion of your land.

RAY. I'm not going to listen to that.

ALICE. Liquidate a portion in order to save part of it.

RAY. In 1956 the cattle market completely bottomed out and then went up $10 a head in a month. If I'd sold out, I'd never have made it back.

ALICE. You're going to lose all of it, Ray.

RAY. No. I'm going to have it all or ... I'm going to have it all.

ETHELYN. How'd you get into this line of work?

ALICE. I don't know. If you'd have told me this is what

I'd end up doing, I'd have said you were crazier than hell. Working for Farmers Home, it was pretty rewarding when I started out. Helping young people get started.

RAY. Living in a city would kill me.

ALICE. No one's asking you to do that—

RAY. —Alice, you don't understand—

ALICE. —Let's just restructure your debt and re-organize your finances.

RAY. This may sound kind of funny and not a whole lot of people are going to tell you this but it's true. Okay. Some people call it nature and I call it nature, too. But it's God really. You get a feeling for God. Even my uncle who's a chicken farmer told me that he feels the presence of God by the growth of his animals. His chickens are parts of God's body that he feeds and tends and he knows God is aware of him because his chickens grow and multiply. See, when you're growing that's creating and it's different from any other kind of creating and you feel it. You feel closer to God. *(He leaves his files on ALICE'S desk.)* You may as well keep all this. I got no more use for it. *(He leaves.)*

ETHELYN. *(Picks up the files.)* I know you're just doing your job. *(Leaves.)*

ALICE. Jesus.

(LIGHTS cross fade. EMIL and WORDY are in Winona's Cafe and Bar.)

EMIL. See, Wordy, it's all changed now. You can hardly hold your head up being a farmer anymore. You want a Coke?

WORDY. Cherry ... I guess...

EMIL. Winona, a cherry cola and a regular Coke, what do you call it, Coke Classic. I don't want any of that new-fangled shit. *(WINONA brings their drinks.)* All the income from my farm operation goes to meet the interest on the money I have borrowed. And that interest clock, it just keeps right on ticking. So, I think you are going to see all the family farms in the hands of a few corporations.

WINONA. And then watch what happens to the price of lettuce.

EMIL. You got that right, Winona, that's for damn sure. Wordy, you want some pumpkin bread?

WORDY. Okay...

EMIL. And another thing that really burns my butt is that you got these politicians who are policy makers. They come and go and they make a two-year commitment or a four-year commitment. And all that time they're setting policy through a farm program or through their relations with foreign countries. And superimposed on top of all that is the fact that politicians are worried about two things:

WORDY. Getting elected and getting re-elected.

EMIL. That's right, and everything else is secondary. And they do those other things to insure those two things, so their priorities are not clear. So, they make a two-year commitment and I make a thirty-year commitment, which means things change an awful lot for me during those thirty years.

WORDY. What are we supposed to do? We can't work any harder, we can't get up any earlier, we can't work any later.

EMIL. What we have got to do is get those goddamn Communists out of the USDA and the Trilateral Commission and do something about that bastard Henry Kissinger because I just know he has something to do with this.

WORDY. What time is it?

WINONA. Ten till two.

WORDY. I've got to go.

EMIL. Don't go.

WORDY. What?

EMIL. I'm talking to you here. Don't you understand? I've got to talk to you. We have got to write our elected officials, Wordy. We can't take this lying down.

WORDY. I've got to meet my dad.

EMIL. Hey, it's all right, no skin off my ass. I'll see you later. *(beat)* You say hi to your dad for me.

WORDY. Thanks for the pumpkin bread.

EMIL. Anytime. *(Pause. WORDY leaves.)*

WINONA. You want another Coke?

EMIL. Dammit, if Lee Iacocca can sell Chryslers, by God, we ought to be able to sell beefsteak.

WINONA. Listen Emil, you've got to throw that John Wayne bullshit out the window. Now, get a computer 'cause they've got mystery. Get a magic bone. Put on your reading glasses. Start managing your business like a business.

EMIL. I am going to write somebody. I've just got to figure out who.

WINONA. How about that Coke?

EMIL. Aw, bring me a beer.

(LIGHTS cross fade. CALEB, WORDY and MAUDALINE are in CARL PRITCHARD'S office at the First National Bank.)

CARL. *(to MAUDALINE:)* Would you like a sucker? I've got lemon and cherry.

MAUDALINE. I'd like lemon. *(He hands it to her.)* Thank you. Can I have one for my friend?

CARL. Your friend?

MAUDALINE. Right here. *(imaginary friend)* My friend, Deena Kay Friday.

CARL. Sure. Lemon or cherry?

MAUDALINE. Let me ask her.

WORDY. She says cherry.

MAUDALINE. She says thank you.

CARL. Tell her she's welcome.

MAUDALINE. My friend Deena Kay Friday can fly through the air. She has been in China and India and Mozambique. Her long shiny black hair floats behind her when she flies. She says that she will teach me how to fly when I am a little older.

CALEB. I got this letter.

CARL. I'm sorry Caleb. It's been recommended to me to take a look at some of our loans.

CALEB. I need to borrow money for next year.

CARL. I can't let you do that. There's no more money.

CALEB. How long have we known each other?

CARL. What are you saying, Caleb? If there's no more money, there's no more friendship?

CALEB. Every year when the first of January goes by I got to have $100,000 to pay taxes and insurance and all this sort of stuff before I can even turn a wheel.

CARL. Farming is a business like any other business, you can only stand so much debt. You've got to sell off, Caleb, pay your debts. You're a well-respected, well-liked knowledgeable cattleman. Go to to work for someone else as a herdsman at a good wage.

CALEB. If I could bail out, I would. The only reason I'm fighting it is that my boy, Wordy, wants to stay with it. And I love this ranch.

CARL. Think about how you're living. I've been to your place.

CALEB. It's been hard since Sarah left.

CARL. The house is full of holes.

MAUDALINE. My friend Deena Kay doesn't have a mommy either.

CALEB. I'm doing the best I can.

MAUDALINE. My mommy went away. I asked her why she was going away. She said we were going to the poorhouse. I asked her where the poorhouse was.

CARL. It's like some shanty, not a house at all. Wordy and Maudaline in ragged clothes.

CALEB. I said, I'm doing the best I can.

MAUDALINE. Then the minister came over to talk to my mommy and daddy. They were talking very loud. Deena Kay Friday and I were watching cartoons so I asked them to either be more quiet or go in the other room. They went in the other room.

CARL. Why beat your head against a brick wall? Go to work as a herdsman. You'll make a good wage, live in a good house, provide an education for your kids.

CALEB. Don't you understand? This is all I got left.

MAUDALINE. My mommy was crying. I asked her what was wrong. She said that she was dying of a broken heart that was breaking in two. I asked if we should call a doctor and she said no. I asked her if she would like my frozen Snickers bar. She told me to leave her alone. I went into the kitchen and climbed on the footstool and opened the freezer and got my frozen Snickers bar and gave it to my mother. She hugged me and then she ate my Snickers bar. I keep Snickers bars around just in case she comes home again. Sometimes I'm afraid to leave the house, because what if she comes while I'm gone?

CARL. Ultimately, the government is going to come along. You know that.

CALEB. I've seen hard times before.

MAUDALINE. We've seen hard times before.

CALEB. *(Stands.)* Come along, Maudaline.

CARL. We're going to have to talk about this soon.

CALEB. Don't you even step one foot on my land.

MAUDALINE. Now she lives in a blue house and rides a red horse at night when the moon has wings. A man with a long beard sits by the river and cries.

CARL. We're going to have to talk about this soon.

CALEB. Don't you even step one foot on my land.

MAUDALINE. The whole sky is popsicle pink and all the children have purple popsicle moustaches. The man with the long beard falls asleep and dreams of his wife who has gone away that he

CARL. I'm very sympathetic to all this. And I do understand. Really. But you have got to be realistic. It's a

loves very much. She is brushing her hair and smells like flowers and wears a lacy nightgown and she is laughing. The man and woman are kissing by the river. They swim in the river. The swim in the river kissing in the river. They find a bowl of apples in the river and they bring them to the old man with the long beard.

business. Back when, you made a decision. Maybe it was a mistake. Maybe it was the wrong decision. Maybe it wasn't. But you're making a mistake now not taking corrective action immediately. You make a decision projecting a particular future, but if you projected that future wrong or that future changes, then you have got to adjust. You can't just keep on hoping. I'm going to have to come out and see you.

CALEB. Then don't come alone. And you'd better bring a bulldozer.

CARL. Jesus, Caleb, our kids are in 4-H together.

WORDY. Not anymore.

CARL. I bought steers from your kids. *(to WORDY:)* Had my picture taken next to you.

CALEB. Come on, Maudaline, Wordy, we're leaving.

MAUDALINE. Can we get ice cream? Dad? Deena Kay Friday and I would like to get ice cream. Can we?

CALEB. Shut up.

MAUDALINE. You never told me to shut up before.

(MOLLY Enters.)

MOLLY. Hi, you guys.

CALEB. Wordy. *(WORDY leaves with them.)*

MOLLY. What's up his ass? *(CARL bends over holding his stomach.)* Dad, you all right? Dad?

CARL. Just give me a minute. Then we'll go get that pizza I promised.

(BLACKOUT)

SCENE 6

SCENE: LIGHTS up. There is a table with a 4-H banner hanging from it. MOLLY sets up for her presentation.

MOLLY. My name is Molly Pritchard of the Golden Wheat 4-H Club and today I'm going to show how to mix shortening and sugar. Okay. First you take the shortening and you measure it. And you've got to level it off with something flat. Like this. And then you put it in a bowl. Like this. Okay. Then you take the sugar and you measure it out. And you level it off. Then you put it in the bowl and then you mix it. *(MOLLY mixes. She looks up. Smiles. Mixes some more.)* And you got to mix it real good to get the lumps out. *(She mixes more vigorously.)* Okay. Is there any questions? I'm not cooking nothing, I'm just mixing. Is there any other questions? Thank you for your kind attention.

MAUDALINE. Why is your dad hurting everybody?

MOLLY. *(startled)* It's not my fault. Is there any other

questions? Thank you for your kind attention.

(BLACKOUT)

SCENE 7

SCENE: LIGHTS up. EMIL holds a head of lettuce and talks to a BUYER.

EMIL. I'm telling you, this is the best crop of lettuce I've ever grown.

BUYER. I can give you 63 cents.

EMIL. It cost me 72 cents a head to grow it.

BUYER. 64 cents and that's my final offer.

EMIL. The one year I don't get hailed out or have a drought. Goddammit, taste this lettuce. It's the finest crop I've ever grown.

BUYER. 64 cents.

EMIL. Now, when you add up planting it, watching over it, picking it, packing it in crates and shipping it to you, it costs me 72 cents a head.

BUYER. 65 cents, Emil, just 'cause we've been doing business for years. I swear to God, though, that's as high as I can go. Take it or leave it.

EMIL. I'll leave it.

BUYER. Then plow it under. *(EMIL throws the head of lettuce to the ground.)*

(BLACKOUT)

SCENE 8

SCENE: LIGHTS up. RAY stands in a field. ETHELYN comes near to him.

RAY. If I'm not a farmer, then what am I? We can't even pay our utility bill.

ETHELYN. Just because things go wrong, doesn't mean you did anything wrong.

RAY. I may not have come from much but I made something of myself. I couldn't believe it when you said, yes, you'd go out with me. I wanted to show everyone that I was worth something. And I took you to Italy for our honeymoon. We walked everywhere. Remember the day we walked up to that small town outside Florence with that castle. And that farmer who shared our lunch. Took us inside a small shed and showed us a statue.

ETHELYN. A beautiful statue.

RAY. He'd plowed up an Aphrodite in his field of artichokes and didn't know what to do with her. If he told anybody, all those archeology types would be crawling and digging all over his farm and he wouldn't be able to raise anymore artichokes. So he kept hiding the Aphordite and every now and then he'd smuggle someone in to have a go at wondering how much could be got for her and the whole thing went on for a year or so. But in the end the farmer buried her in the field again and he went back to raising artichockes. So, every field I see, I think of an Aphrodite buried under it. I think that there is magic beneath the soil. Imagine. Finding Aphrodite buried in your field and not knowing what to do with her.

(FADE OUT)

SCENE 9

SCENE: LIGHTS up. JOHN sits at a desk working over a pile of papers. He's lit by the glow from a small desk lamp. We hear the click-click-click of an adding machine.

In another area, TESS and WINONA henna their hair and drink daiquiris. A RADIO plays softly. TESS hums along. She's no longer pregnant.

TESS. Here's your daiquiri. *(WINONA sits in a chair smoking. TESS stands over her working on WINONA'S hair. TESS' hair is already done up in a henna cap with pieces of her hair poking up through the holes in the cap. TESS finishes pulling WINONA'S hair through the cap.)*
WINONA. Last month my hair turned a little orange.
TESS. Then we won't leave it on as long this time.
WINONA. You're in charge.
TESS. How do you think I'd look with black hair?
WINONA. What kind of black hair?
TESS. Like Annette Funicello.
WINONA. Who?

TESS. You know, Annette Funicello, the one with the ears.

WINONA. (*shakes head.*) no.

TESS. The mouseketeer).

WINONA. Sorry.

TESS. You don't know the mouseketeers? The Mickey Mouse Club? Monday was "Fun With Music Day." Tuesday, "Guest Star Day." Wednesday, "Anything Can Happen Day." (*WINONA shakes her head.*)

WINONA. I think I need a cigarette. (*She lights up.*)

TESS. Do you want another daiquiri?

WINONA. Yes.

TESS. I'll make another pitcher. Stop picking at your hair. (*TESS leaves. WINONA smokes her cigarette.*)

WINONA. (*off to TESS.*) Yesterday, I saw a white cat somersault backwards down Crawson Street. You don't believe me. It's true. (*WINONA stands. She is very still. There is a shift in spirit like the levitation. TESS enters with the daiquiris. She stops and looks at WINONA.*)

TESS. Winona?

WINONA. Tess.

TESS. Are you all right?

WINONA. Come with me this year.

TESS. I'll think about it.

WINONA. You say that every year. (*The "levitation" moment passes.*)

TESS. Here's your daiquiri.

WINONA. (*Remembers henna cap.*) It's been ten minutes. I think we're done. (*They take off the henna caps and rub their hair with towels.*)

TESS. Well?

WINONA. What do you think? (*They look closely at each other.*)

TESS. Do we look any different?

WINONA. Not really. (*beat*) I feel different, do you?

TESS. Yeah.

WINONA. You will think about it, won't you?

TESS. I'll think about it.

(JOHN still works at his papers. A small light. The sound of an ADDING MACHINE.)

(FADE OUT)

SCENE 10

SCENE: LIGHTS up. JOHN at his desk. The rustle of papers, the click-click-click of an ADDING MACHINE.

TESS comes outside. It is an hour or so later than the previous scene. TESS looks at the sky.

JOHN takes a break and comes outside. He holds a few of his papers.

JOHN. It doesn't look so good.

TESS. What? My hair? What about it?

JOHN. No, not your hair. *(He looks at her hair.)* Why, did you do something to your hair?

TESS. Sort of.

JOHN. What are you looking for?

TESS. I want to see Halley's Comet.

JOHN. They say you get a better chance if you stand on your head.

TESS. Oh, come on.

JOHN. No, really, I read it in *National Geographic. (She squints her eyes at him.)* I'm serious.

TESS. Oh, John.

JOHN. You don't believe me? I'll go first then. *(Stands on his head.)* Oh ... mmm...

TESS. What? What?

JOHN. Oh, yes...

TESS. What John? Do you see something?

JOHN. You better come look, Tess.

TESS. *(Stands on her head.)* Where? I don't see anything. *(He knocks her over, tickles her, they fall over laughing.)*

JOHN. You are so dumb. Did you see it, Tess? Huh? Huh?

TESS. Can't believe I'm out here standing on my head with you. You know, I think I did see something for just a moment. *(Pause. A quiet moment. They both look at the sky.)*

JOHN. Remember the summer we built the house and every day you made us lunch and we rode out to the field in the pickup and had a picnic and listened to the radio. One afternoon "Lara's Theme" from *Dr. Zhivago* came on the radio and I asked you to dance with me. I remember how we couldn't dance real close 'cause your belly was all swollen up with Margaret Anne. *(pause)* Honey, I'm so so sorry.

TESS. I want to move the baby.

JOHN. You can't move a grave.

TESS. It's not a grave, she's Margaret Anne.

JOHN. It's against the law.

TESS. No one will care.

JOHN. Why do you want to move our baby?

TESS. I want to make sure a part of me is here. That way, they don't win, I win. I'm dug in. Whatever grows, I'm part of it.

JOHN. Do you blame me?

TESS. No.

JOHN. Talk to me, Tess.

TESS. What about?

JOHN. *(not irritated)* I don't know. Things. Who you think is going to win the World Series, whether we should have hamburgers for dinner, what color you'd like to paint the kitchen.

TESS. I'd like to paint the kitchen yellow.

JOHN. Okay, I like yellow.

TESS. I'm losing my family's land.

JOHN. But, Tess, we married. It's all mixed together.

TESS. No, you don't understand. My father left this to me.

JOHN. Whatever is happening is happening to the both of us.

TESS. No, it's different. You married into this. I was born into it.

JOHN. You know I have always done my best by you and your family.

TESS. *(Holds up John's papers.)* You think this lets you own land. Pieces of paper.

JOHN. Yes, I do believe I can do something with these pieces of paper.

TESS. It's all over, don't you see? It's all slipping away. I'm losing it for my dad.

JOHN. What are you saying? That we should just let it all go?

TESS. Yes, just let it go, John. *(She turns to leave. He stops her.)*

JOHN. No, don't leave yet. *(pause)* I miss you, Tess. I miss you. *(He touches her hair.)* I always liked the color of your hair. Auburn. *(He kisses her hair.)*

TESS. I can't.

JOHN. It's been long.

TESS. I'm sorry.

JOHN. Tess?

TESS. I have to go now.

JOHN. Please, Tess.

TESS. I have to go get all my things and bring them to one place.

JOHN. Don't leave me. *(She's already gone. JOHN goes back to working on his papers.)*

(FADE OUT)

SCENE 11

SCENE: A starry night. Lots of silences. Something very beautiful. A night out of a Chagall painting where lovers fly through the air and girls die of broken hearts. A carefully woven tapestry of the entire community. Lighting will vary to focus the action.

AT RISE: TESS goes and gets her things and gathers them in a barrel. Old photographs, ribbons, packets of sequins, a collection of baseball cards, a stack of 45's. ALICE stands in her office, barefoot with her pants rolled up. ETHELYN and RAY are in a field. RAY sits in his pickup. CARL, JOHN, WINONA and EMIL are in WINONA'S Cafe. EMIL is writing letters. MOLLY and WORDY lie on a hill looking for Halley's Comet.

ETHELYN. Ray?

MOLLY. Is this the best place?

ETHELYN. Ray?

MOLLY. You're supposed to be on a hill.

RAY. Prego, Etalina.

MOLLY. You're supposed to be on a hill to get the best chance of seeing Halley's Comet.

WORDY. We're on a hill.

MOLLY. I know that.

RAY. Here is my passport. Ecco il passaporto.

ALICE. Bill.

BILL. What happened?

ALICE. Don't step there. It's all sticky. *(BILL takes off his shoes and socks and rolls up his pants.*

ETHELYN. I brought you dinner.

RAY. What do you want? Che cosa desidera?

ETHELYN. You can't sit in that truck forever.

MOLLY. Wordy?

WORDY. What?

MOLLY. Nothing. *(pause)* I might go away somewhere. *(She juggles three small balls.)*

WINONA. Is he going under?

CARL. Caleb is one helluva chore man. He'll chore 'till midnight, but he's never been much with a pencil.

WINONA. Shit.

EMIL. Got to start managing your business like it was a business.

ALICE. Someone's poured maple syrup all over my office.

BILL. Lucky I brought pancake mix.

JOHN. Your business suffering?

WINONA. I've got nothing to do all day but drink cherry cola, chew gum and smoke Camel cigarettes.

EMIL. Dear Senator, All my life I've been a conservative. I believe in the true American way of life.

ETHELYN. Do you want this?

RAY. Dov' e l'autobus de va in centro di Firenze?

ETHELYN. Remember Nathan's red Cherokee tractor? *(ETHELYN stays with RAY eating the dinner herself.)*

MOLLY. I might want to be a clown.

WORDY. Why is your dad hurting everybody?

MOLLY. What?

EMIL. You got any pumpkin bread left?

WINONA. Yeah, a piece.

EMIL. Dear Congressman, All my life I believed if you work hard and have determination, you'll excel financially.

WORDY. My mom said we're going to the poorhouse. My sister asked where the poorhouse was.

JOHN. I got your letter, Carl.

MOLLY. People borrowed that money. Nobody made them do it.

RAY. I have a letter of credit. Ho una lettera di credito.

ALICE. I don't think this floor has been scrubbed in years.

JOHN. I filed Chapter 11 today.

WORDY. My dad says bankers are a different kind of person, you know what I mean?

MOLLY. No, I don't know what you mean.

EMIL. *(to JOHN:)* Write your elected officials. That's the way to correct any injustice or unlivable situation.

WORDY. Did you hear about this new kind of tractor they got out?

MOLLY. No.

WORDY. It doesn't have a seat or a steering wheel. It's for farmers who've lost their ass and don't know which way to turn.

RAY. Do you have a telephone directory for Rome? Ha un elenco di Roma?

ETHELYN. Why are you talking in Italian?

RAY. Just let me be.

MOLLY. Do you think that glow is it?

JOHN. I filed Chapter 11 today.

MOLLY. Wordy, have you ever had a girlfriend?

WORDY. No.

MOLLY. Do you ever think about it?

WORDY. No.

MOLLY. Me neither.

WINONA. How's Tess?

WORDY. My dad won't hardly come to town anymore.

JOHN. My father-in-law won't come to town anymore.

ALICE. *(to BILL:)* People who've worked their land for generations and someone like me tells them it's not good enough. Well, that's the end of everything they worked for and it's not 'cause they weren't working hard. They were till all hours. *(She gets down on hands and knees and scrubs her office floor.)*

JOHN. He blames me. *(to BILL:)* Tess won't talk about it. She doesn't seem angry, she doens't seem upset or disappointed. She doesn't seem anything at all. And I feel like a bomb is about to go off and no one will talk to me.

(NOTE: When people turn to BILL, they are alone with him.)

WORDY. I want to be a cattleman. And if I don't have that land, I can't ask you to marry me.

MOLLY. Who says I'd marry you if you had a bizillion acres of land? What in hell are you talking about, anyway?

WORDY. If you can't understand, I don't see how we can go on being friends.

MOLLY. Fine.

WORDY. Fine.

MOLLY. That's just great. Why don't you piss off. *(She juggles and keeps hitting WORDY with the balls.)*

WORDY. Quit it.

RAY. I'm sorry, I don't understand. Mi dis piace, non capisco.

CARL. Jesus, John, I'm real sorry about all this.

EMIL. All my life I heard that if we had problems to contact our elected officials.

CARL. I don't understand what's going on.

RAY. These aren't my shoes. This isn't my laundry.

CARL. *(to BILL:)* And I don't know how to stop it from happening. When I bought this bank, my accountant told me I wouldn't have any trouble unless interest rates passed 17% and we had a good laugh over that one.

WINONA. I like you Carl. I've always liked you. But I'd rather shovel shit than do what you do for a living.

EMIL. I shovel shit.

CARL. This situation involves a lot more people than the farmer and the farmer is all you're hearing about. There are bankers who've lost their banks, there are bankers who've lost their lives.

WINONA. Seems like you could do something.

EMIL. Write your elected officials.

CARL. I'm just trying to do my job as best I can. That's all.

WINONA. Then stop doing your job.

RAY. *(to BILL:)* See, I knew exactly what to do and I knew exactly the right way to do it and I did everything exactly as I was supposed to and I need for you to tell me I'm not crazy.

BILL. *(to RAY and ETHELYN:)* It's a phase. That's all. There is this phase and then there is the next phase. And you've got to get through all the phases. And when you've gotten through all the phases, that's a life.

WORDY. I like your dad.

MOLLY. That's great. I'm so happy I could shit. *(She starts to cry. A sob escapes. WORDY hugs MOLLY.*

(A falling STAR.)

WORDY. A falling star. Make a wish.

MOLLY. I wish that pigs could fly so I could make a fortune selling umbrellas. *(pause)* Wordy, do you believe in God?

BILL. *(alone)* They just shut off the water and lights in my church.

WORDY. I don't know.

MOLLY. I believe God is everywhere but losing.

BILL. They just shut off the water and lights in my church.

JOHN. I feel like this bomb is about to go off.

EMIL. Start managing your business like it was a business.

ETHELYN. Ray, come on inside.

RAY. I'm doing the best I can, Ethelyn.

ETHELYN. Come inside and talk to me.

RAY. It doesn't do any good to talk.

ETHELYN. I'm afraid. I don't know what's going on with you. We've had hard times before.

WORDY. We've had hard times before.

MOLLY. I want to go away from here.

RAY. I want to think about things that are nice. Like *Tosca.* There is no way to be sad while thinking about *Tosca.* Where is the opera house? Dov' e il teatro dell'opera? *(BILL moves to be with ALICE.)*

ALICE. Do you hear that music? *(There is nothing we can hear.)* When I was a little girl I danced for my father. I had a little pink jewelry box that when it opened a tiny ballet dancer twirled and pirouetted and my dad would say, "Dance for me Twinkle Toes."

BILL. Dance, Alice. *(She does. BILL holds her arm while she pirouettes. MOLLY and WORDY kiss. RAY starts dancing.)*

ETHELYN. Why are you dancing?

RAY. Because I hear this music inside my head.

(FADE OUT)

SCENE 12

SCENE: TESS has not moved from the previous scene and may still be sitting with her collection of things while everyone else moves off. TESS' nightmare. TV game show MUSIC swells.

ANNOUNCER. Ladies and gentlemen, gentlemen and ladies, boys and girls. The judges have arrived at their decision and a very hard decision it has been. All of the farm families this year were superior ones, but as the good book says, many are called but few are chosen. Would you give your warmest welcome and your biggest round of applause for the 1986 Farm Family of the Year. *(loud cheers)* TESS AND JOHN HARPER, COME ON DOWN.

(TESS and JOHN rush down from the audience holding hands and looking happy and excited. Crowns are put on their heads and banners flung across their chests reading, "Farm Family of the Year.")

ANNOUNCER. And do we have some really wonderful prizes for you, Tess and John Harper. A year's supply of Wonder Woman pantyhose. *(Cheers.)* A two year supply of lemon flavored Jello pudding. *(Cheers.)* A three-year supply of Jumbo Cheeze Doodles. *(Cheers.)* Brand new hand-tooled genuine Ranchero cowboy boots. A 26 inch Sony Trinitron color television. A brand spanking new Ford Bronco. A complete set of Louis Vuitton luggage.

And look in that front zip pocket, little lady. What do we have here? Your foreclosure notice. Ha ha ha ha. *(He hands them the envelope and runs off. They open it and read it together. John leaves. TESS stands holding the notice. She slowly removes the crown and the "Farm Family of the Year" banner. TESS floats up in the air ever so slightly.)*

(FADE OUT)

SCENE 13

SCENE: Sunset. A field.

AT RISE: TESS holds the foreclosure notice. She floats in the air, levitating. Again, suggest the levitation with LIGHT and MUSIC and by having TESS separate from the other women. Perhaps even at a height from them.

TESS. Why doesn't anyone call me anymore? No one calls me. No one calls John. The telephone never rings.

(ETHELYN is in the field hitting a head of lettuce with a stick while speaking Italian.)

TESS. You know why I think it is? People are afraid. They're afraid to be near failure like it's a disease and it could be catching. We like the good, the strong, the successful, but we steer clear of the failures. They must've done something very wrong or they wouldn't be in this terrible predicament, would they? *(ETHELYN consults RAY'S Italian phrasebook and practices a line over and over.)*

(From off, we hear MOLLY and WINONA baying at the moon like mad wolves. ETHELYN hears them. MOLLY and WINONA Enter. They are howling and wailing at the gods and having a raucously good time. The three women look at each other, caught in a moment of odd behavior. It is cold and all the women are bundled up in mitts and hats.)

ETHELYN. Winona? Molly? Are you two drunk?

WINONA. We came out to bay at the moon.

MOLLY. And look for Halley's Comet.

WINONA. *(Juggles three small balls.)* What are you doing out here?

ETHELYN. I'm learning Italian so I can talk to my husband.

WINONA. Italian?

MOLLY. *(laughter)* Buon Giorno. Pizza. Lasagna. Ravioli.

WINONA. You've got to hold yourself together, Ethelyn. That's what you want to do.

ETHELYN. Hold *myself* together? I'm not the one out here baying at the moon.

WINONA. No, you're just wandering through a field at night hitting a head of lettuce with a stick and speaking Italian. *(MOLLY wails at the moon some more. ETHELYN laughs at the ridiculousness of it all and bays at the moon a couple times herself.)* Get a pedicure, hang a snake on a fence and take care of yourself. If Ray is going to lose his shit, you've got to hold your own life together.

ETHELYN. Where do you get that kind of stuff? Out of magazines? We're not people in magazine articles. Out here a person's life isn't a series of big events to be applauded or booed, but a slow accumulating of days and seasons and years.

WINONA. It's just that I want to shout at someone and where are the people we should be shouting at? *(beat)* In four months we've lost Hellman's lumberyard, the Red Owl grocery...

MOLLY. ...the Allis-Chalmers dealership and Hildegard implements...

ETHELYN. Time was we had three farm implement dealers,

MOLLY. a movie house,

WINONA. two car dealers,

MOLLY. a rollerskating rink,

WINONA. a fortune teller,

ETHELYN. a creamery,

WINONA. a dancehall...

ETHELYN. Oh, God, every Saturday night we had such dances. You remember those, Winona?

WINONA. All those dances.

ETHELYN. Oh, remember that time Patsy Cline came to sing at the County Fair? You might not be impressed, Molly, but Patsy Cline was big stuff. *(WINONA strikes a pose, leans her head slightly back, closes her eyes and sings a damn good rendition of Patsy Cline singing "Your Cheatin' Heart,"**

*See Cautionary Note, page 3.

joined first by MOLLY and then by ETHELYN, as they finish, they collapse, breathless, laughing.)

WINONA. Does anyone have a cigarette?

MOLLY. I do.

ETHELYN. You do? *(The three women have a smoke together. ETHELYN looks up.)* Do you think that glow is it? *(They look up. WINONA senses something. Spirit.)*

TESS. Winona and I were riding down Route 50 and there was Bill Hoddupp. He'd pulled his car over to the side of the road and was sitting on the hood staring out over the field.

WINONA. I hear there were only eight in church last Sunday.

TESS. He was on his way to a meeting to discuss the church situation when he pulled over to the side of the road. He said he wanted to climb out onto the hood of his car and stand there and freeze to death. I said that I would come with him to the meeting and he said, "Why bother? Where there is no vision, the people perish." And Winona said, "That's horseshit. We've been going along for centuries with no vision and here we all are."

MOLLY. My grandmother says, God is air and just by breathing in He becomes us.

WINONA. Close your eyes.

MOLLY. What?

WINONA. Shhh. Spirit. Listen. Hear It whistling through the leaves.

TESS. Take me. Take me.

ETHELYN. Please let something good happen to Ray soon.

TESS. I think maybe we are more alive when people

say we are dead than we are now.

WINONA. Here It, whistling through the leaves.

TESS. I keep having these dreams where everyone is floating. Their bodies are all airy and see-through and I am longing so badly to be weighted down but every time I take a step, I float up to the clouds. I push my cart down the aisles of the grocery store and all these bodies float past me. In the dream, I am looking for things to weigh me down. We do all sorts of things to give our lives this feeling of weight. We try to get good grades in school, fall in love, nurse our children through chicken pox. And we think that these things mean something and that piled together they add up to a life and surely that means something. But the things we grab onto to weigh us down are so airy that we just float away. *(TESS drops the foreclosure notice to the ground. Then she takes off her watch, her earring, her wedding ring and drops them. TESS floats away.)*

(JOHN comes in. He finds TESS' jewelry and the foreclosure notice.)

BROADCASTER'S VOICE. In local and area news today, a farmer in eastern Colorado killed herself. Tess Harper, a farmer despondent about her family's mounting financial woes, committed suicide Wednesday by climbing atop a barrel of burning trash the day after her family's wheat crop was harvested. Harper, whose family had farmed since 1910, hated the idea of losing the farm, said her brother, Robert Ferguson. "She felt that she had failed her parents, her family." Harper, who would have been 34 today, was overcome by smoke, police said. Her body was discovered by her husband, John Harper, who said he also found a note indicating his wife's concern about finances and her intention to take her life. When asked what he would do now, John Harper said, "I don't know. When you're in the last bloody ditch, there's nothing left to do but sing." *(JOHN holds the foreclosure notice. He takes out a match and lights it on fire. He holds the burning paper in his hand until he has to let it go. Then he drops it to the ground.)*

MOLLY. I'm running away to Clown College in Sarasota, Florida. *(JOHN holds TESS' jewelry and sings "Red River Valley.")*

(LIGHTS CROSS FADE)

SCENE 14

AT RISE: JOHN sings "Red River Valley" a second time. People begin setting up wooden benches. It is TESS HARPER'S funeral. Everyone assembles in the Full Gospel Lighthouse Church. BILL HODDUPP stands holding a Bible.

BILL. In the words of Solomon: "All the rivers run into the sea; yet the sea is not full; unto the place from whence the rivers come, thither they return again." Everyone here knew Tess Harper. Everyone here loved Tess Harper. We are very sorry that she is gone. We shall miss her.

We shall mourn her. This morning I would like to address myself to those who are left behind to carry on. I take for my text Matthew 14, verses 22 - 32.

And straightway Jesus constrained his disciples to get into a ship, and to go before him unto the other side, while he sent the multitudes away.

And when he had sent the multitudes away, he went up into a mountain apart to pray: and when the evening was come, he was there alone.

But the ship was now in the midst of the sea, tossed with waves: for the wind was contrary.

And in the fourth watch of the night Jesus went unto them, walking on the sea.

And when the disciples saw him walking on the sea, they were troubled, saying, It is a spirit; and they cried out for fear.

But straightway Jesus spake unto them, saying, Be of good cheer; it is I; be not afraid.

And Peter answered him and said, Lord, if it be thou, bid me come unto thee on the water.

And Jesus said, Come. And when Peter was come down out of the ship, he walked on the water, to go to Jesus.

But when he saw the wind boisterous, he was afraid; and beginning to sink, he cried, saying, Lord, save me.

And immediately Jesus stretched forth his hand, and caught him, and said unto him, O thou of little faith, wherefore didst thou doubt?

And when they were come into the ship, the wind ceased.

And that's where the story usually ends, with Peter's lack of faith. And it becomes a lesson about how we should have faith in times of trouble. Well, that's not what I get from the story. Peter stepped out of the boat into the storm and walked on the water to Jesus. I don't read anywhere in that story or anywhere else in the Bible that any of the other disciples stepped out of the boat into the storm. Only Peter. Peter may have panicked in the moment but he was the only one with enough faith to step out of the boat and experience walking on water with Jesus for even a small moment. Small moments of faith.

See, I believe that the best this world has to offer are those small, rare moments when we experience something like "walking on water." We all seem to be dwelling on our failures and the things we may have done wrong. I feel that at times, too.

Most of you know that this is the last time this church as a building will be open. But a church is not a building. It is not the brick and the wood. A church is its people. I have to believe that God is calling us forth to be used in some way that we may have been preparing for all our lives. We have to step out of the boat. *(pause)* Let's all join hands and remember Tess Harper.

(The community joins hands. The REPORTER, NEWS DI-RECTOR and CAMERAMAN come through the crowd and begin the next scene. The community stays onstage posed at the funeral.)

(LIGHTS CROSS FADE)

SCENE 15

*SCENE: The editing room of a TV station, part two. The RE-
PORTER, NEWS DIRECTOR and CAMERAMAN and
their Twinkies, coffee cups and french fries.*

DIRECTOR. Okay, we'll end the piece with that lyrical
blizzard stuff. You know, the end of a way of life and all
that. Other than that, we'll stick to the suicide and
funeral. Okay? Let's see the visuals around the
suicide.

REPORTER. We don't have any specifically related to
the suicide.

DIRECTOR. You don't have any? But that's the story.

REPORTER. No one got it.

DIRECTOR. What do you mean, no one got it?

CAMERAMAN. The husband was real protective.

REPORTER. We couldn't even get close to the house.

DIRECTOR. No burning trash? Smoking embers?
Nothing around the house? Something to do with the
woman? I need a visual angle.

REPORTER. I said, no one got it.

DIRECTOR. So all you got is all this talking head
stuff?

REPORTER. I like it.

DIRECTOR. I can't run the story without some visuals.
The rest, I mean, it's nice, don't get me wrong. But it just
doesn't grab me.

REPORTER. I think the real story is what is happening to the community. How they're coping. What they think. How this suicide affects them.

DIRECTOR. But it's got no "sex." We've got to have some visuals or else we can't run it. You know that. I'm sorry. *(long pause)*

CAMERAMAN. Well, is that it?

DIRECTOR. Yeah.

CAMERAMAN. Wanna catch the end of the game? We could go to Sid's.

DIRECTOR. Yeah, I ought to. I've got five bucks on the game.

CAMERAMAN. *(indicating reporter's sandwich)* You going to finish that?

REPORTER. Take it. Take it.

CAMERAMAN. Hey, here's an extra ketchup. My lucky night.

DIRECTOR. Goodnight.

REPORTER. Night. *(The CAMERAMAN and NEWS DI-RECTOR leave. The REPORTER taps a pencil on the desk. The REPORTER runs back through some of the "clips.")*

EMIL. Dammit, if Lee Iacocca can sell Chryslers, by God, we ought to be able to sell beefsteak.

MAUDALINE.
God is great
But we have to wait
To see if everything is A-okay.

CARL. My daughter, Molly, ran away. She's 14. Here's a picture. Maybe you could help.

WORDY. *(from the Future Farmers' creed)* "I believe that to live and work on a good farm or to be engaged in other agricultural pursuits, is pleasant as well as challenging. For I know the joys and discomforts of agricultural life and hold an inborn fondness for these associations which, even in hours of discouragement, I cannot deny."

JOHN. She got this big smile and her hands just opened at her sides.

CALEB. You really ought to live a year out here. It's a romantic kind of thing. You're out there battling the elements all the time. Winds blow through that you wouldn't believe. Blizzards with 60 mile-an-hour winds, snow driving straight this way killing hundreds of thousands of cattle. Lightning storms with bolts of lightning that looked as wide as my car. Hail softball size. We had one hail storm that the hail wasn't that bad but it was driven by a 60 mile-an-hour wind. A field of corn beaten to the ground. Then you got to have the rain at the right time. If it doesn't rain at just the right time, you can lose your whole crop. It's a way of life. It's a delightful way of life. (The REPORTER is alone with these ghosts.)

(The LIGHT slowly fades)

SCENE 16

SCENE: Late night. A field. A flurry of snow.

AT RISE: BILL is barefoot with his pants rolled up. He's drunk, *wandering about the field, laughing, looking for something.*

BILL. Is it here? No, that's not it. Is that it over there? Nope.

CARL. Bill? *(BILL runs across the field.)* Bill, what are you doing?

BILL. Shhh. Looking for my church. *(He laughs, staggers, and rushes off to another spot.)*

CARL. You'd better come with me.

BILL. Ahh, Carl, hope I freeze to death.

CARL. Come on, we'll go to Winona's. Get you some coffee.

BILL. You will tell me, won't you?

CARL. Tell you what?

BILL. If you see it.

CARL. What?

BILL. My church.

CARL. Yes, I'll tell you.

— *END OF ACT I* —

ACT II
SCENE 1

SCENE: We hear the intro MUSIC for the CBS Evening
News.*

    *LIGHTS up on WINONA'S Cafe. CARL is trying to get
BILL sobered up. They drink coffee and watch the news.*

"DAN RATHER". *(V.O.)* In national new today, David
Stockman, Director of the Office of Management and
Budget, appeared before the Senate Agriculture Com-
mittee.

"STOCKMAN". *(V.O.)* I cannot figure out why the tax-
payers of this country have the responsibility to refinance
bad debt that was willingly incurred by consenting adults
who went out and bought farmland when the price was
going up and thought that they could get rich.

"DAN RATHER". *(V.O.)* Commenting on Mr. Stockman's policies is economist Dr. Harry Lippman.

"LIPPMAN". *(V.O.)* The free market is economic Dar-
winism. At least Darwinian biologists acknowledge the
violence of competition. These political Darwinians
insist that the free market benefits both predator and
prey. So Mr. Stockman can suggest that the bankruptcy

---

*See Cautionary Note, page 3.

of thousands of farm families is merely the working of a "dynamic economy" which will compensate their losses by creating new jobs elsewhere, say in Silicon Valley..

That these failures and successes are not happening to the same people, or even to the same groups of people, is an insight beyond Mr. Stockman. By his reasoning, the richness of the rich justifies the poverty of the poor.

"DAN RATHER". *(V.O.)* This is Dan Rather saying good-night for the *CBS Evening News.* Courage. *(Repeat the CBS music.)*

BILL. Did he say courage? What's that supposed to mean?

CARL. He's been signing off that way lately.

BILL. What's it mean?

CARL. Well, how about that hard little stare he does when he finishes every news item, a sort of a call-me-a-liar stare.

BILL. What's that mean?

CARL. I think the stare is what comes of growing up Texan and sensitive at the same time.

BILL. What does courage mean?

CARL. He says it's simply one of his two favorite words in the English language.

BILL. I guess that's the Texan side of Dan Rather.

CARL. His other favorite word is meadow. *(They start to giggle, enjoying each other's silliness.)*

BILL. I guess that's the sensitive side of Dan Rather.

CARL. Imagine what it would've done to the national pysche if he'd ended the evening news, "This is Dan Rather," hard little stare, "meadow."

BILL. People all across America would be spitting out

their Tater Tots, Cheeze Whiz and jello in shock, blurting, "Meadow? Did he say meadow? What in hell did he mean by that?"

CARL. You want another cup of coffee?

BILL. Yeah. *(beat)* Meadow? *(They laugh together.)*

(BLACKOUT)

SCENE 2

AT RISE: ETHELYN sits alone in a bit of LIGHT. She telephones the Rural Crisis Hotline.

ETHELYN. Hello? I didn't know if somebody would still be up this time of night. I've called you before but hung up as soon as someone answered the phone. I'm not really calling for myself. I know you can't come out here and talk to my husband and he won't come in to town and talk to you. I've just eaten 14 pieces of cinnamon toast and I'm not feeling very well. Ray would be angry if he knew I called you. I feel I'm being kind of disloyal, but I can't think of anyone else to talk to. Ray is sitting out in the middle of our pasture in the pickup truck. I asked him what he was doing and he said, "Ethelyn, this whole thing has got pressure on my mind. Got pain on left side."

My brother in Detroit has helped us make some of our

payments, and Ray feels that he has lost all of his pride and he can't even provide for his own family anymore. I don't really understand what's happening. Three years ago we were worth three million dollars, at least that's what they told us, and two weeks ago they came and took our cattle away. I don't know. One thing I do know is that for every loser, someone is winning somewhere.

Lately he's got this book and a tape recorder with him in the pickup. I can see him talking away. I asked him what he was doing. He said, "A long time ago, I made a pledge to myself that I would die bilingual." He is learning Italian. He is sitting in the middle of a pasture in a pickup learning Italian.

Tonight? I've been looking at our family photo album. There's a picture of Nathan, my littlest boy, riding his toy tractor down our driveway. His Cherokee tractor. He can't be more than four years old. It's a beautiful sunny day, and Nathan is surrounded by light. The whole photograph shimmers like a highway in the desert on a hot, hot day. The older I become, the more I am drawn to light, radiance of all kinds.

I know I'm not alone. I watch the news. I saw all of the Dan Rather series about the end of the family farm. I never thought I was watching my own life story. We can't pay our utility bill this month. He's 56 years old. What kind of a job is he going to get?

Someone name me the day we stopped being good

ranchers and started mismanaging. He's a good man. He made this ranch work. We bought this land 23 years ago. It was rundown non-producing land. We turned it into land that produced good lines of Red Angus cattle. Red Angus so fine that buyers would wait for Ray's livestock to go on the market. They would come from all over the state to buy Ray's yearlings. I am proud of him. I think my husband has done very well. He's worked hard all these years to build up his bloodline. You can't just replace that kind of quality

My friend Sarah Stratman told me it's kind of like facing being an alcoholic. You've just got to stand up and say it. Well, we are broke. That's all there is to it. We are plain broke.

I drove up to Lewisville today. It's about an hour's drive from here. Not so many people around there will know me. Besides, there's just not much work around here for someone like me.

I'm 52 and I've never before in my life filled out a job application. I pulled in to this Burger Bonanza outside of Lewisville. I said to them that I would very much like to have a job there. So this young man, young enough to be my grandson, in fact, everyone in this place was young enough to be my grandchild. So this young man gave me a job application to fill out. I couldn't answer half of the questions. My life didn't fit on their application. But I answered it as best I could. Then this same young man asked me what size I wore, and I said that I generally wore about a size 10. Then he said to me, "Mrs. Mac-Cormick, you could start Monday if you would like." I said that I would like that and thanked him very much and drove back home. I tried on my uniform. It's orange and brown. Fits all right.

There's a woman who lives in here, Winona Tarlow. She's Hopi Indian. Every year she goes with some other women to the ancient Indian cliff dwellings in Mesa Verde to pray for balance. I'm thinking this year maybe I might go with her.

I think what you're doing here with this Rural Crisis Hotline is a real good thing. Thank you. Goodnight.
(ETHELYN puts on her Burger Bonanza hat. It's orange and brown.)

(FADE OUT)

SCENE 3

AT RISE: LIGHTS up on a graveyard at night. WINONA sits at TESS' gravesite wearing a henna cap, drinking from a thermos of daiquiris. She is interrupted by a noise.

WINONA. Who's there?

(JOHN Enters.)

JOHN. Winona?

WINONA. What do you want?

JOHN. It's Tess's birthday.

WINONA. Go away.

JOHN. I brought flowers.

WINONA. I'm having my own private party.

JOHN. Do you mind if I join you? *(silence)* I've got as much right, I've got more right to be here than you do. *(pause)*

WINONA. Hear you got a new job. Property Management Consultant.

JOHN. That's right.

WINONA. What kind of a job is that, exactly?

JOHN. I manage properties.

WINONA. And how exactly do you manage those properties?

JOHN. I manage properties that have been foreclosed on for the Federal Land Bank. I act as the middleman between the farmer and the bank. *(pause)* I needed a job.

WINONA. Sounds real peachy. *(Looks around noticing something missing.)* Where's Margaret Anne?

JOHN. Tess wanted to ... we moved her. *(pause)* What's in the thermos?

WINONA. Daiquiris.

JOHN. Mind if I have one?

WINONA. Why not? *(He takes a swig and passes it back to WINONA. She pours herself another.)*

JOHN. You know, I miss her, too. *(WINONA looks away.)*

You want to know what my job is like, what it's really like? It's shit. I get to escort people off their property. Okay? But you know the way the system works and the kind of debt a lot of farmers are in, it is well within the right of the Federal Land Bank and a normal business procedure to foreclose, take the collateral and try to sell it. I'm just trying to help that happen as expeditiously and sensitively as possible. And my own personal situation is my father-in-law won't talk to me. And that's what's left of my family. He hasn't come to town for over a year. He says I've crossed over.

WINONA. I'm sorry, John.

JOHN. Maybe I'm not doing the right thing. But I'm doing what I'm doing because I needed to do something about what was happening. I am just trying to survive, you know.

WINONA. I know.

JOHN. Remember how she got this big smile on her face and her hands just opened at her sides?

(TESS appears.)

WINONA. Yes. *(pause)*

JOHN. What's that on your head?

WINONA. Oh, shit, shit, shit, it's been way over 10 minutes. *(She yanks off the henna cap and her hair is a little orange.)* Don't even tell me.

JOHN. What color do you call that?

JOHN. It's a little orange. *(They laugh together.)*

WINONA. *(Raises a daiquiri.)* Happy Birthday, Tess.

JOHN. *(Raises thermos.)* Happy Birthday, Tess. *(TESS*

smiles.) Growing up, we never thought of it as a business, we just liked counting cows.

(LIGHTS CROSS FADE)

SCENE 4

AT RISE: The distant THUNDER of an approaching storm echoes. RAY is looking at the sky.

ETHELYN is returning from work. She carries her purse and keys and wears her Burger Bonanza uniform.

ETHELYN. Ray, I'm home.

RAY. The sky's turning yellow.

ETHELYN. A hailstorm. I don't believe it. That is almost worth a smile. I suppose it doesn't matter anymore. *(pause)* You coming in?

RAY. In a minute.

ETHELYN. *(She feels a raindrop.)* It's starting to rain. Ray?

RAY. Ecco il passaporto.

ETHELYN. You're going to keep disappearing in little bits on me, aren't you? Damn you. I won't forgive you. *(Silence. He looks away.)* You coming in? I'll wait for you at the top of the hill. Ciao. *(She leaves him. He watches her walk off.)*

(LIGHTS CROSS FADE)

SCENE 5

AT RISE: Night. ALICE and BILL are taking calls at the Rural Crisis Hotline. They are both on the phone. BILL listens to his caller with the occasional, hmmm, uh huh, etc. ALICE talks to her caller. We don't see or hear this caller.

ALICE. *(on phone)* I do think you should call Mrs. Hendricks at the Center ... You don't need to be embarrassed. I've been through the Stress Management Seminar myself ... All different kinds of people ... It made me feel less alone ... *(BILL hangs up his phone.)* ... No, you don't have to say anything if you don't want to ... Give Mrs. Hendricks a call. Okay? ... I'll give you a ring next Monday just to remind you ... You're very welcome. *(ALICE hangs up. She logs her call.)* Ten till twelve. Almost the witching hour.

BILL. Alice? *(Pause. Awkward. She looks at him.)* How long can you keep this up, working all day at the FHA and here four nights a week? Are you tired?

ALICE. Does a bear shit in the woods? Is New York big? *(beat)* For awhile longer. It helps me most. Okay.

(The PHONE rings.)

ALICE. Right on time. *(She answers.)* Rural Crisis Hotline.

EMIL. *(on phone)* Yeah. Anybody 'round there happen

to take a look at the goddamn newspaper today? Sonuvabitch, I'm sorry, but I have to say it again, sonuvabitch. You call those cattle prices? What are those goddamn communists at the United States Department of Agriculture doing to us? They must be selling us all down the river to the Russians. When we get to the bottom of all of this horseshit international banking conspiracy we are going to find the name of that bastard Henry Kissinger once again. *(BILL looks at Alice, questioning. She covers the mouthpiece with her hand and says, "Yup, it's him.")* I am telling you, I have lost all respect for our elected officials. I've been to Washington. I've seen how the government works, and if I had the opportunity right now, I would drive my tractor back to Washington, I would walk up to the President of the United States and say, "Hey, what is going on around here? You got your thumb in your bum and your mind in neutral, buster." *(to a dog off:)* Lay down! Shut up and lay down! I'll feed you later! See, you can write a polite letter trying to get some information from the USDA and all they say is, I'm sorry, but that department has been abolished, I'm sorry but we don't keep those records anymore. Well, I'll be goddamned sorry myself but I am tired of paying their salaries. They are not getting another tax dollar out of me. They can send me straight to hell or jail. Just what in hell are they doing to us? They sure ain't helping no farmers, I can tell you that for a fact and the whole damn thing just pisses me off sideways. Uh, thank you very much. Bye.

ALICE. Goodnight, Emil. *(She hangs up.)* He was in top form tonight. I think he's getting worse.

BILL. Sometimes I feel I'm going to the cupboard and the cupboard is bare.

ALICE. Are you worried?

BILL. Do fat babies fart?

ALICE. I fear I'm a corrupting influence on you. You mind if I smoke?

BILL. No.

ALICE. How did you ever get mixed up with such a vice-ridden sinner as me?

BILL. All preachers' daughters—

ALICE. Preacher's daughter?

BILL. Isn't that what you are? All preachers' daughters are vice-ridden and have a wild streak. That's what my daddy told me.

ALICE. Oh, yeah, and what else did your daddy tell you about preachers' daughters?

BILL. Oh, that you could catch them smoking cigarettes and drinking whiskey behind the church most Sunday evenings during the service.

ALICE. *(smiling)* Oh, yeah, and what else?

BILL. That they can give you an awful good romp in the back seat of a car.

ALICE. *(Shrieks, throws cigarettes, styrofoam coffee cups, crumpled paper, whatever at BILL)* I don't believe you. I wonder how your daddy knew all that stuff.

BILL. Anything else stick from being a preacher's daughter other than the cigarettes and whiskey?

ALICE. Like what? I can still name all 66 books of the Bible in order. Is that what you mean?

BILL. Not really.

ALICE. You mean, do I believe? I respect your faith.

Really, I do. I'm envious of it. I wish so bad sometimes I still had something solid like that in my life to hang onto. It just stopped working for me a long time ago. So, I've learned not to depend on the Lord and I'll make the changes myself.

BILL. I don't really believe that.

ALICE. The thing I really can't forget are all those old hymns. There's something so good and solid and true about them. And no matter where I go and who I am, they still stay somewhere deep in my gut.

(The PHONE rings.)

BILL. My turn. *(He picks up.)* Rural Crisis Hotline.

CARL. Bill? Is that you?

BILL. Well, hi, Carl. How are you? *(ALICE picks up the stuff.)*

(LIGHTS up on CARL.)

CARL. I've been cleaning out my office tonight. I just have the rest of the week. The house is all packed up. *(CARL is standing holding the phone. He wears his basketball sneakers and holds his uniform on a hanger. Near him is a cardboard box full of things.* Uh, I guess it's kind of late.

BILL. Not late around here.

CARL. No, I guess not. Well. I got all the pictures off the wall and all the stuff out of my desk. This here's a photograph of me giving the prize for the best decorated bicycle in the Fourth of July parade. And this is me in one of the uniforms I donated to the basketball team when they went to the Regionals. This is the cowboy hat Caleb gave me to wear to my first rodeo. *(beat)* I brought all the pieces of my dream together here, and then it all went wrong. *(beat)* You know, those boys could go to State this year. Last year's whole starting line-up is returning this year and I hear that Floyd Burns grew two inches over the summer.

BILL. Remember that shot Floyd made with two seconds to go in the Sectional Final?

CARL. Oh, it was a pretty shot wasn't it?

BILL. Those boys go to State, I expect to see you in the stands rooting for them.

CARL. If you would send me any clippings about the team care of the Bismarck Motel, I would sure appreciate it.

BILL. You'll come back to visit?·

CARL. Oh, sure. North Dakota's not that far.

BILL. I mean it.

CARL. Anyone hears from Molly, you'll let me know?

BILL. We sure will.

CARL. I don't know where she is, Bill. My daughter's run away. Not even a postcard. I don't even have that.

BILL. I understand.

CARL. Well, I'd better go. You take real good care of yourself, Bill. *(He hangs up. LIGHT fades out on CARL.)*

BILL. You, too, Carl. *(BILL hangs up.)*

(There is a faint GLOW in the sky.)

BILL. Alice, come outside. I think I see Halley's Comet. *(ALICE has fallen asleep.)* Alice? *(BILL touches her hair.)*

(FADE OUT)

SCENE 6

AT RISE: It is a cold, wet night. JOHN and CARL come to escort CALEB, WORDY and MAUDALINE off their property. MAUDALINE plays hopscotch.

MAUDALINE.
I scream
You scream
We all scream
For ice cream.

JOHN. Hi, Maudaline. How are you? *(No answer. She continues playing.)* Would you do us a favor and run tell your daddy that we're here to see him?

MAUDALINE. Daddy, Daddy, they've come for the cows again. *(CARL and JOHN wait.)*

CARL. Looks like chance of rain. *(CALEB stands in darkness and shines a FLASHLIGHT on CARL and JOHN.)*

CALEB. *(from a distance)* What do you want?

JOHN. I think you know why we're here.

CALEB. Make it short.

JOHN. By order of the district court, the Federal Land

Bank has authorized the county sheriff to forcefully remove you from your property tomorrow morning at 8 a.m., place all your belongings on the road, and take your cattle for collateral. Caleb, the bank has authorized Carl and me to escort you off your place tonight and avoid a real mess tomorrow morning.

CARL. We brought a pick-up and as many loads as it takes, we will take all your belongings into town. We've got you a motel room reserved.

CALEB. Now, let's get a few things straight. For one, all my cows are dead.

WORDY. We poisoned them.

(CALEB and WORDY step out of the darkness. CALEB holds a gun.)

CALEB. And two, I'm not going anywhere. So, why don't you all get off my land. *(pause)* I said, get off my land.

JOHN. You don't own this land anymore.

CALEB. This is my land. And right now you're on it only because I'm allowing it. You understand?

CARL. We understand.

JOHN. There are deeds, contracts. You signed them.

CALEB. I don't give a good goddamn about any contracts.

CARL. It's already cold, Caleb. How are you going to make it another winter in that house full of holes?

CALEB. Who asked you to comment?

WORDY. You're the ones trying to starve us to death.

CARL. Why don't you go to work as a herdsman for

someone else? It's good money and you've got a lot of valuable knowledge to sell.

CALEB. That's right. I've got a lot of knowledge. I worked hard all my life for that knowledge and what's it gotten me? I did everything by the book, obeyed all the rules. And just what has all that valuable knowledge gotten me? At my age, a herdsman for some snot-nosed kid.

CARL. Your kids are in rags.

CALEB. You doing so damn well yourself, Carl Pritchard? Your girl's run off, God knows where. So don't be telling me about the speck in my eye when you got a log jam in your own.

CARL. Why are you doing this?

CALEB. I don't need you to understand why. I already took this through the courts in the proper fashion. I haven't made a lot of noise. Tried to proceed with some dignity. See, I don't care much for those radical type farmers carrying signs and yelling slogans. I've kept my mouth shut.

JOHN. Caleb, you don't have a lot of choices here. You can leave here quietly tonight with us or have a real ugly scene tomorrow morning.

CALEB. How's your father-in-law, John? Haven't seen him in awhile. *(pause)*

JOHN. Okay. That's fair. You want to say I've got a leg on each side of the fence. Well, that's fair, too, but I'm just running a business, Caleb, and whether or not you believe me, I am trying to help.

CALEB. Bullshit.

JOHN. We have managed to keep you on your land as

long as we could.

CALEB. Oh, sell it to some other asshole, will you?

JOHN. Let's go, Carl, we've done all we could. *(angrily turns on CALEB)* It's all on paper, Caleb. Deeds, contracts. You signed them. We all did. And we're all paying for it. So, get on with it. *(Sails a piece of paper at CALEB.)* Here's your court order.

CARL. *(Steps toward CALEB.)* Caleb, give me the gun.

CALEB. *(He points it at CARL.)* Don't you step one inch closer.

CARL. We were friends, Caleb, good friends. *(pause)* I thought we could still be friends.

CALEB. Well, we can't.

(CARL takes another step forward. CALEB whips the gun up and SHOOTS it toward the sky. Everyone freezes.)

CALEB. Now, you all listen to me. Don't tell me anymore about deeds and contracts and pieces of paper and how I am bound by them because I do not care. I will break whatever laws and rules are necessary. Now, get off my land.

WORDY. Shoot 'em, Daddy, shoot 'em.

CARL. I'm real sorry about all this. *(CARL and JOHN leave.)*

MAUDALINE. Can we get ice cream now, Daddy. You said.

(CALEB puts down the FLASHLIGHT. He turns around slowly and slams the butt of his gun across MAUDALINE'S face. She jerks back and falls to the ground. Nobody moves. WORDY stands

*with his mouth open. CALEB walks into the darkness. WORDY
runs to MAUDALINE.)*

WORDY. Maudaline? Maudaline? Hey? Sing it with
me. I scream, you scream, we all scream, for ice
cream.

MAUDALINE. *(Says a couple of the words. She struggles to
stand. She stands wobbly on her feet. She turns around slowly,
arms outstretched.)* I'm flying, Wordy. I'm flying.

WORDY. Where are you flying, Maudaline?

MAUDALINE. I'm flying inside. I'm flying inside. *(Shift to
WORDY'S dream.)*

WORDY. Hello? Hello? Operator? Get me the White
House. That's right. I don't care what time it is. I am
Wordsworth Stratman, I am 15 years old, I am an
American, and I need to talk to the President. My sister's
been — Hello? Mr. President? This is Wordsworth Stratman calling long distance. Well, I am not well, thank you
very much, I am not well at all. I helped kill all our cows.
Molly's run away. Emil's in a slaughterhouse. No, I don't
think you really do understand. You're forgetting about
us, and we're still out here. We're people and we're still
out here. We haven't gone away. My mom's gone away.
My dad sits by the river and cries. Hey? Are you listening
to me? I am getting myself a lawyer and I am suing the
U.S. Government for bringing this evil upon my family. I
just thought you ought to know 'cause my sister's been
hit in the head. Hey? Mr. President, if God sees the little
sparrow fall, does He see me? Does He?

(The LIGHT fades on WORDY and MAUDALINE.)

SCENE 7

AT RISE: LIGHTS up on the Rural Crisis Hotline. Late, late night, almost morning. BILL is on the phone with someone. CALEB telephones. He's sitting alone in the dark.

ALICE. Hello, Rural Crisis Hotline. How can I help you? *(pause)* Hello? *(pause)* It's all right. You don't have to talk if you don't want to. We've got lots of time. *(pause)* Can you tell me why you called? Can you tell me your name?

CALEB. *(Whispers.)* I can't tell you my name, because I don't want to bring anymore shame on my family than I already have, and, besides, it is my name. And if I ever think I'm strong enough to get out of here, then I'd like to just leave this place behind and all my reasons for putting myself in here. So ... just call me "no name" because I don't deserve a name. I've lost it.

ALICE. Okay. Do you want to tell me about it?

CALEB. I'm here because of my eight year old daughter. She's my youngest. See, it was her birthday. She knew money was tight and all she asked was to go to Del Tulle's in town and have an ice cream sundae with those little colored sprinkly things on top. That's all. And I'd promised her. Well, when she asked me, and she asked me real nice, I put down my flashlight and I turned around and I slammed the butt of my gun right across her face.

85

Then I walked back up to the house and sat down right then and there and called Mrs. Patrick Hendricks — she's the lady who works at the Center — and told her I wanted to commit myself to the State Hospital because I'd lost every shred of hope and decency I'd had.

See, I'm not a farmer. I'm not a businessman. I'm not a Christian. I'm not a father. I'm not a man anymore. So, the next day I came here. *(CALEB quietly hangs up the phone. ALICE puts down the phone, shaken. BILL comes over and holds her. She rests a hand on his arm.)*

ALICE. Do you remember the day the Space Shuttle Challenger exploded? It was one of the most remarkable days of my life. Everywhere you went that day, people had their TV's on. Tens of thousands gathered around those boxes of light watching the Lord take those seven in a twinkling. We kept watching those scenes of kids in school gymnasiums watching Christa McAuliffe blow up. It must have been 50 times. The light from the TV's reflected on our faces. I was shopping and this little boy held my hand and cried, "Why didn't they have any parachutes?" And this woman turned to me and said, "I felt very close to her. She was ordinary people. She was a mother, a working woman." And it seemed right that I should hug this woman in a shopping mall. I know it was a disaster but it was a great day for us. Those TV's connected us almost as though we'd linked hands stretching across the county. I remember the seven astronauts and Christa McAuliffe, but what I remember most about that day was that something terrible happened to *us* and *we* cried out.

BILL. "Two are better than one; because they have a good reward for their labor. For if they fall, the one will lift up his fellow: but woe to him that is alone when he falleth; for he hath not another to help him up. Again, if two lie together, then they have heat: but how can one be warm alone?"

ALICE. Ecclesiastes 4:9-11. See, some of being a preacher's daughter stuck. *(BILL pulls ALICE slowly up to him. He pushes her hair back from her face, brushes the tears from under her eyes, touches her nose, her lips. Holding her face in both hands, he tips it up to his and kisses her.)*

(FADE OUT)

SCENE 8

AT RISE: EMIL and WORDY are sitting at a table in WINONA'S. George Jones plays on the jukebox. "I've Aged 20 Years in 5."* EMIL works in a slaughterhouse now and he wears a huge white bloodied smock. He pours two shot glasses of Jack Daniels to the rim. Hands one to WORDY. EMIL downs his and pours another. WORDY sips his.

EMIL. You can't beat George Jones.
WORDY. 'Cause he understands.
EMIL. That's right. And you know to keep an eye on

* See Cautionary Note, page 3.

this Henry Kissinger fellow.

WORDY. Yes.

EMIL. Okay now. What time is it?

WORDY. *(Looks at EMIL'S watch.)* 2 a.m.

EMIL. If you've got to go, I'll understand.

WORDY. No, I'm all right.

EMIL. Did you know that pigs get bored? Well, they do. When they're all scrunched together in a small pen with no stimulation, they can get kinda squirrelly. So, if pigs get bored, what about me? Aren't I supposed to be a few rungs up the ladder from a pig? You know what kind of a job I got now? Killing animals all day long. You ever smell the inside of a slaughterhouse? It isn't pretty. *(pause)* See, Wordy, we live in a world that exists.

WORDY. You got your beginnings and you got your endings.

EMIL. That's right. You can't escape along the way. That's over. Can't. Dead cows far as your eye can see. Working that hammer. Suddenly, you find yourself in a situation where, like, that's the way it is. Slaughterhouse. You can't get out of it.

WORDY. Why don't you sell off a piece of land, Emil.

EMIL. There's always that impulse towards another kind of world. Something that doesn't necessarily confine one so much. See, I speak English, have gestures, wear a certain kind of clothes, but once upon a time I didn't have any of that shit. *(Downs a second shot glass and pours another.)* What did you say?

WORDY. Why don't you sell off a piece?

EMIL. Here's a quarter, *(He drops change on the floor.)* go put something on the jukebox. *(EMIL kneels on the floor picking up his change. WORDY picks* "Still Doin' Time"* *by George Jones. He comes back and helps EMIL up.)* Good choice.

(BLACKOUT)

SCENE 9

AT RISE: CARL works in a motel. He's listening intently to a basketball game on the radio.

RADIO. Number 10, Dale McGrab, his pivot foot looked like it moved, oh, there's the whistle, he's called for travelling, ball in the opposite direction.

CARL. Damn.

RADIO. A sloppy pass by number 16 on the North Central team—

CARL. —Get it, get it.

RADIO. —and Floyd Burns intercepts the ball.

CARL. Go, Floyd.

RADIO. And he's dribbling down the court, passes off to number 21, Harrison Hoppenfeld. The Central team has switched to its man-to-man, and the ball is back to number 4 Floyd Burns at the top of the key. And he's up and there's the shot ... and it's good. *(CARL raises his arms*

---

*See Cautionary Note, page 3.

and cheers.) There's the buzzer. Halftime. And it's 42
to 42.

(The TELEPHONE rings. CARL turns the radio down some.)

CARL. Bismarck Motel, can I help you? ... It's $42.42, I
mean $33.50 ... uh huh ... checkout time is 11 a.m. ... oh,
sure, we take American Express...

(MOLLY Enters.)

CARL. ...so that's two for the fourteenth...
MOLLY. Daddy?
CARL. *(He turns, holding the phone.)* Molly.
MOLLY. I couldn't find you.
CARL. I had to move.
MOLLY. Winona told me.
CARL. Where have you been?
MOLLY. *(She puts on a red nose.)* I've been a clown.
CARL. Lord, haven't we all.
MOLLY. Want to see a picture of me?
CARL. *(Looks at the photo.)* That's the saddest clown face
I've ever seen. *(pause)* You've come home?
MOLLY. You run away and join the circus and it takes
every dime you earn getting back home again.
CARL. You know, Floyd Burns grew another two
inches while you were gone.
MOLLY. Jesus.

(BLACKOUT)

SCENE 10

*SCENE: A Farm Auction/Thanksgiving dinner at the MacCor-
mick place. At the same time, in the same place. Two worlds.
Each entirely real and full unto itself. The worlds are
simultaneous, co-existing with a constant shifting of focus.
One world doesn't freeze while the other takes over.*

*AT RISE: The Thanksgiving Dinner. A warmly lit place.
ETHELYN, WINONA MAUDALINE, RAY, WORDY
and JOHN sit round a table sharing Thanksgiving dinner.
There is a child's small record player near them.*

*Table setting: table and cloth, 6 chairs, a small Venetian
glass centerpiece, 2 candlesticks, 6 plates, cutlery, 6 glasses,
a turkey on a platter, bowl of dressing, cranberry jelly, gravy
boat, yams with pecans and marshmallows, green beans
and a basket of rolls.*

*The Farm Auction. Bright, unkind early morning LIGHT
on the auctioneer standing behind the podium. Carrying
clipboard, paper and forms, JOHN works as clerk for the
auction. He is also present at the dinner. There are TWO
WORKERS from the Emmerling Auction Service helping.
JOHN is the only person in this scene in both worlds shut-
tling back and forth between the two. He doesn't inhabit the
two worlds in the same time, but is fully in one world, and
then fully in the other.*

RAY comes in and out of awareness of both of the worlds but physically he stays in the Thanksgiving dinner.

AUCTIONEER. Okay, let's get started.

ETHELYN. I'm glad you're all here with Ray and me on Thanksgiving.

JOHN. As a representative of the Federal Land Bank, I have been granted the authority to open this public sale of property on this Thursday the 27th of November, nineteen hundred and eighty-six, in the year of our Lord.

ETHELYN. I've set a place for Emil, but I don't know whether he'll be able to make it.

WORDY. He's in Denver selling some land.

WINONA. Is he going to have anything left?

WORDY. Some.

JOHN. Looks like he might make it.

WORDY. I'm going to go work for him.

ETHELYN. He could get here later. We'll save him a plate.

WINONA. Let's give thanks for this wonderful feast Ethelyn has laid out for us.

ALL. Yes.

ETHELYN. Wordy, would you like to say the blessing? *(They stand, join hands and bow heads praying silently.)*

JOHN. This sale will be conducted by the Emmerling Auction Service.

AUCTIONEER. The Emmerling Auction Service holds no responsibility for any accident that might occur.

(ALICE Enters holding a pie.)

JOHN. State and city taxes will be charged to the buyer and no property can be removed until settled for.

ALICE. Sorry I'm late.

ETHELYN. We're just glad you could make it.

WINONA. Where's Bill?

ALICE. He couldn't get away. We get a lot of calls on holidays. He asked me to give you this pumpkin pie. He made it himself.

ETHELYN. You tell him thank you, and we'll send him a plate of food over to the Hotline.

MAUDALINE. We were going to say grace. *(ALICE joins the circle. So does JOHN.)*

WORDY. Dear God, be close to us on this Thanksgiving Day. Be close to others who should be here but aren't. I am thankful to be here today, healthy, with my friends, good friends, eating good food prepared by good people and being in this warm kitchen. Amen.

ALL. Amen. *(They sit. The dinner begins with the passing of food, pouring of drink, talk and laughter. JOHN returns to the auction.)*

JOHN. Ethelyn MacCormick has asked me to read the following: "We have decided to quit farming and offer the following property at auction." And it's signed, Ethelyn and Ray MacCormick. *(pause)* The sale is now open.

AUCTIONEER. We'll start with farm machinery. Item number 1. *(He continues auctioning quietly. In the rest of the scene, when the auction isn't the focus, the AUCTIONEER continues auctioning pieces off and we see them carried away.)*

WINONA. I was thinking about everyone who was here last year.

ETHELYN. Carl and Molly should be with us.

JOHN. I got a postcard from the motel. Carl's coaching junior high basketball.

WORDY. What's he know about managing a motel?

JOHN. I imagine he'll learn.

AUCTIONEER. Sold.

ALICE. The table, the food, it all looks beautiful, Ethelyn.

AUCTIONEER. Item number 2. *(JOHN picks up turkey and platter from the table. Holds it up.)* A 1974 Massey-Ferguson 1505 tractor, four-wheel-drive, new 3208 turbo Cat engine, 88 hours on the engine, a cab and air conditioned. *(JOHN carries turkey over and hands it to one of the Emmerling workers. He returns to the dinner. In the rest of the scene, JOHN picks up the objects from the table, carries them to a worker standing next to the auction podium, and returns to the Thanksgiving dinner.)* Start the bidding.

ALICE. Are these pecans in the stuffing? Ray would you like some? *(He doesn't answer. ALICE looks at ETHELYN. She nods. RAY doesn't eat or speak during scene but people serve him food on his plate.)*

AUCTIONEER. Sold to the man in the red cap. *(A WORKER carries the turkey off.)*

MAUDALINE. I love yams with marshmallows and brown sugar.

WINONA. Bascially, Maudaline, that's what yams are all about, a good excuse to eat melted marshmallows and a lot of brown sugar.

AUCTIONEER. Next item. Two John Deere drills, 8-foot-10-inch spacing, like new. *(JOHN picks up the plates of yams and green beans carrying them over.)* Who'll start the bidding? *(pause)* They're in mint collection.

WINONA. I got some pictures back the other day of the bowling tournament. *(to WORDY:)* There's some great ones of your dad. I thought you might like to see them. *(She passes them around.)*

AUCTIONEER. Anybody? Well, let's put those drills aside for a bit. *(WORKER carries yams and beans off.)*

JOHN. Next? *(JOHN holds up basket of rolls and takes to podium.)*

ALICE. Who took this picture from behind, *Winona?* Look how big my butt looks.

AUCTIONEER. A New Holland 277 baler, string tie, VH 40, Wisconsin engine. Who'll begin?

MAUDALINE. Would you pass the gravy, please?

WORDY. I like the uniforms.

WINONA. They do look sharp.

ETHELYN. Not as sharp as mine.

AUCTIONEER. Come on, somebody make me an offer. This farm machinery is in excellent condition. John assures me that the MacCormicks take real good care of their machinery.

ALICE. Carl donated the uniforms.

AUCTIONEER. How about you, sir? Saw you eyeing that baler earlier.

WINONA. There's one of Tess.

MAUDALINE. There's us cheerleading, Winona.

AUCTIONEER. This farm equipment is not moving.

ETHELYN. There's Caleb bowling the winning strike.

JOHN. Maybe we better go on to something else.

WINONA. You can keep them, Wordy, if you like.

AUCTIONEER. Okay, you all are just going to make it

hard on me for awhile. You don't like farm machinery?
Okay. Well, how about a little joke, lighten things up a
bit. What's the difference between heart disease, cancer,
syphilis and farm machinery? You can't get rid of farm
machinery. Ha ha ha ha ha.

JOHN. We'll move on to smaller farm equipment
and livestock.

AUCTIONEER. Item number 1. A bushel bin scale.
*(JOHN holds up bowl of dressing and gravy boat and carries it
over to worker and returns to his chair.)* Who will start the bidding? *(AUCTIONEER quietly auctioneers.)*

ALICE. I'll take a little more of that cranberry jelly.

JOHN. *(Sits at table. to WORDY:)* When's your dad coming home? *(silence)*

MAUDALINE. Pretty soon.

ETHELYN. Would anyone like more turkey?

WORDY. *(to JOHN:)* How do you "sensitively" escort
somebody off their property?

AUCTIONEER. Sold, to the little lady in the parka. Now,
here's some real nice bridles, halters and tack. *(JOHN
picks up the cranberry jelly and two candelsticks.)* Sold.

JOHN. We're moving on to household goods. *(Gathers
up the glasses from the table.)*

AUCTIONEER. Let's start the bidding for this loveseat
with hand-stitched tapestry pillows.

JOHN. Oh, no, these are their personal things.

AUCTIONEER. It's all going, John. It's their collateral.
You know that. You signed the papers. Sold.

WINONA. I don't know, John. One of the ways I think
about this whole situation is, us and them. And I'm not
sure anymore if you're an us or a them.

JOHN. I'm just trying to keep experts on the land. I don't care so much if they own that land. I want to keep them as stewards of the land.

AUCTIONEER. A woman's oak rocker, handcarving on the arms.

JOHN. Please, please stop. These are their personal things. *(Gathers up cutlery.)*

MAUDALINE. Last night I had this dream where my friend Deena Kay Friday and I had this bicycle boat. It was a bicycle-built-for-two bicycle boat, and we were peddling near some island and it was warm and blue and people in canoes paddled out to us and little children walked in the water to give us armloads of bananas.

WINONA. It is good to dream of bananas.

AUCTIONEER. A child's red Cherokee wagon.

JOHN. $54.19. *(This is how much JOHN has in his pocket. There is a pause. JOHN gathers the plates.)*

AUCTIONEER. All right, John.

ETHELYN. I'm so full I could bust.

WINONA. It was all wonderful.

WORDY. Maudaline has memorized a poem to recite as a way to say thank you and give a small gift back.

MAUDALINE. It's by Emily Dickinson.

AUCTIONEER. Let's start the bidding on this collection of carnival glass from Venice. *(JOHN collects the chairs.)*

WINONA. Maudaline needs a stage. *(WINONA holds the centerpiece. A WORKER yanks off the tablecloth and carries it off. They help her up to stand on the table.)*

MAUDALINE.
'Twas just this time last year I died.

I know I heard the corn,
When I was carried by the farms,
It had the tassels on.

I thought how yellow it would look
When Richard went to mill
And then I wanted to get out,
But something held my will.

I thought just how red apples wedged
The stubble's joints between;
And carts went stooping round the fields
To take the pumpkins in.

I wondered which would miss me least,
And when Thanksgiving came,
If father'd multiply the plates
To make an even sum.
    AUCTIONEER. A glass ball-footed antique table. *(JOHN
holds up the small Venetian glass centerpiece.)*
    MAUDALINE.
And if my stocking hung too high,
Would it blur the Christmas glee,
And not a Santa Claus could reach
The altitude of me?

But this sort grieved myself, and so
I thought how it would be
When just this time some perfect year,
Themselves should come to me.
    AUCTIONEER. Sold. *(JOHN drops the centerpiece and it shat-*

ters. He picks up the pieces of glass.)

ALL. *(clapping)* Bravo, Maudaline. *(She dances on the table while they clap.)*

AUCTIONEER. And finally, the last item, a brass liver oil lamp.)

(WORKERS come to carry the table over. MAUDALINE leaps from the table.)

ETHELYN. Let's have pie and coffee in the parlor. Ray, why don't you put on some music. Ray?

RAY. I didn't come from much, but I made something of myself. *(He Exits.)*

ETHELYN. Alice, I'll have a plate up for you to take to Bill. *(All but JOHN and MAUDALINE leave. She walks over to where he's picking up the pieces of the Venetian centerpiece.)*

JOHN. That was a lovely poem, Maudaline.

MAUDALINE. Why are you crying?

JOHN. I don't know.

MAUDALINE. Maybe you should talk to God.

JOHN. Religion is difficult, you know.

MAUDALINE. We're all journeying to where God is, aren't we? *(Both Exit.)*

AUCTIONEER. Sold. Well, that's it boys. Let's all go home. *(The table is carried off. AUCTIONEER carries podium.)*

(The stage is bare except for the record player. The stage DARKENS. There is a small circle of LIGHT around the record player.)

SCENE 11

SCENE: The stage is bare except for the small record player. A small circle of LIGHT surrounds the record player. RAY steps into the light holding a rifle in each hand. He is alone. He turns on the record player. "Tosca" plays. The great tenor aria from "Tosca." The MUSIC swells louder and louder. A bright white LIGHT shines on RAY. The MUSIC ends. He stands there a moment holding the guns. BLACKOUT. RAY Exits.

Silence.

We hear a voice calling from off.

ETHELYN. Ray? Ray?

(A beam of LIGHT cuts across the stage. ETHELYN comes in carrying a FLASHLIGHT.)

ETHELYN. Oh God oh God Ray where are you? *(She searches with the flashlight and comes upon the record player. A cry escapes from her throat. She holds the light unsteadily on the record player.)* Please, please no. *(She waves the flashlight all about the darkness looking for Ray. (weakly)* Ray? Ray? Ray MacCormick answer me. *(She cries softly and continues looking for her husband.)*

(From the other side of the stage comes a beam of LIGHT. ETHELYN points her flashlight into the oncoming beam of light. RAY Enters carrying a FLASHLIGHT.)

ETHELYN. *(Cries out in relief.)* Where ...?

RAY. I put the guns in the river. *(ETHELYN rushs toward him. They kiss each other hungrily, each drinking the other in, tasting tears and salt. Laughing and crying, they hold each other hard and close.)* Thank you for waiting at the top of the hill.

(BLACKOUT)

SCENE 12

SCENE: A starry night. The "Gift Event."

AT RISE: WINONA sits on a cooler and smokes.

WINONA. Dan Rather has been and gone. Willie Nelson has been and gone. Gary Hart has been and gone. Jessica Lange and her movie, "Country," been and gone, although folks around here don't call that a movie, they call it a documentary.

Every year about this time I go with some other women to the ancient Indian cliff dwellings at Mesa Verde to pray for balance. We have a butterfly event, a crazy dog event, a gift event, and a vision event.

A circular, roofless enclosure is built of willow poles. Across the top run a series of parallel strings along which many yellow butterflies, cut out of mountain-sheep skin, are hanging. A singer sits at the center of the enclosure. As she sings, she beats on an inverted basket with one hand, scraping a stick a foot long on it with the other. This makes the butterflies look as though they were fluttering, dancing in time to her tune.

Act like a crazy dog. Wear sashes and other fine clothes, carry a rattle and dance under the butterfly tent singing crazy dog songs after everybody else has gone to bed.

(PEOPLE come to the gift event. Someone carries a blanket, someone a thermos, someone a cooler. And they sit in a circle.)

WINONA. Sit in a circle. Start by giving away different colored glass bowls. Have everyone give everyone else a glass bowl. Give away handkerchiefs and soap and teddy bear candies and things like that, or pretend to do so. Pretend to be different things. Talk Chinese or something. Give away a frying pan saying things like, "Here is this frying pan worth $100 and this one worth $200." Give everyone a new name. Give a name to a grandchild or think of something and go and get everything.

(Amidst the stars, there is one area that has a faint GLOW that increases in brightness in the scene.)

WINONA. Tess, here is this henna cap worth $49.
WORDY. Molly, here is this umbrella worth $99.
ETHELYN. Alice, here is this red Cherokee tractor worth $97.

ALICE. Ethelyn, here is this wrist corsage worth $44.

EMIL. Winona, here is a magic bone worth $9.49.

MOLLY. Dad, here are these basketball sneakers worth $164.

CALEB. Carl, here is this cowboy hat worth $235.

TESS. John, here is this record of "Lara's Theme" worth $83.

MAUDALINE. Dad, here is an ice cream sundae worth $14.

CARL. Ray, here is this Venetian carnival glass worth $2.53.

RAY. Wordy, here is this Italian phrasebook worth $1.98.

EMIL. Bill, here is a church worth $1 million.

BILL. Alice, here are these ballet slippers worth $314.

RAY. Ethelyn, here is this artichoke worth $600.

WINONA. Sit in a circle. Say your name and something that is on your mind. *(beat)* My name is Winona Tarlow and I'm thinking about how much better I like Emil than John Wayne.

JOHN. My name is John Harper and I'm thinking about how I miss the Full Gospel Lighthouse Church.

WORDY. My name is Wordy Stratman, and I'd like to get a computer.

ETHELYN. My name is Ethelyn MacCormick and I'm considering running for mayor.

CALEB. My name is Caleb Stratman and I'm thinking about Sarah.

TESS. My name is Tess Harper, and it's easier to leave than to come back.

BILL. My name is Bill Hoddupp and, Ray, you're not crazy.

EMIL. My name is "Emil the Fifth" and Wordy, I'm thinking about that night we listened to George Jones songs till sunrise.

MAUDALINE. My name is Maudaline Stratman and I'm real glad my dad is out of the hospital.

CARL. My name is Carl Pritchard and for some reason the only thing on my mind is:
Hey diddle diddle
The cat and the fiddle
The cow jumped over the moon
The little dog laughed
To see such sport
And the dish ran away with the spoon.

ALICE. My name is Alice Darke and I was remembering dancing for my father. He called me "Twinkle Toes."

MOLLY. My name is Molly Pritchard and I wish I didn't wear glasses.

RAY. My name is Ray MacCormick and I'm thinking about people with lights all around them. How can they see the stars?

(The sky GLOWS a little more brightly.)

WINONA. Pretend to be someone else. *(pause)* I am Ida, Caleb's aunt, and I miss you playing the saxophone.

JOHN. I am William, Ethelyn's date for the prom. We won first place in the dance contest. Remember, we danced the foxtrot.

WORDY. I am Emil the Seventh, Emil the Fifth's grandson, and I'm glad you sold off that piece of land.

ETHELYN. I am Sarah, Maudaline's mother, and I love frozen Snickers bars.

CALEB. I am still Caleb and I can't pretend to be someone else at this stage of my recovery.

TESS. I am Annabel, Molly's best friend, and I like your glasses.

BILL. I am Frances, Alice's mother, and Alice, that Bill is a nice guy.

EMIL. I am Peter, and Bill, you're right, the rest of the disciples were a bunch of goddamned chickenshits.

MAUDALINE. I am Margaret Ann, Tess and John's daughter, and I love you once, I love you twice, I love you more than beans and rice.

CARL. I am Jack, Ethelyn's campaign manager, and I think you'd make a terrific mayor.

ALICE. I am Isabella Rosario, Ray's friend, Prego, Ray, dove si trova la casa Michelangelo?

MOLLY. I am Muriel, Winona's sister and *(Sings.)* "Your cheatin' heart will tell on you."

RAY. I am Sam, Bill's little brother, and thank you for teaching me how to throw a curve ball.

WINONA. Give back to someone a saying or poem. *(pause)* I am Winona, and Tess, who's the leader of the club that's made for you and me?

JOHN. I am John, and Emil, if Lee Iacocca can sell Chryslers, by God, we ought to be able to sell beefsteak.

WORDY. I am Wordy, and Molly, I wish that pigs could

fly so we could make a fortune selling umbrellas.

ETHELYN. I am Ethelyn, and Ray, every time I see a field I think of an Aphrodite buried beneath the soil.

CALEB. I am Caleb, and Maudaline, maybe Deena Kay Friday will teach me how to fly when I am a little older.

TESS. I am Tess, and John, they say you get a better chance if you stand on your head. I read it in *National Geographic.*

BILL. I am Bill, and Carl, meadow.

EMIL. I am Emil, and Wordy, you have your beginnings and you have your endings.

MAUDALINE. I am Maudaline, and John, we're all journeying to where God is, aren't we?

CARL. I am Carl, and Bill, Jesus said, Come. And when Peter was come down out of the ship, he walked on the water.

ALICE. I am Alice, and Bill, do fat babies fart?

MOLLY. I am Molly, and Dad, let's go get that pizza you promised.

RAY. I am Ray, and Maudaline, God is great, but we have to wait, to see if everything will be A-okay.

(It's becoming very BRIGHT overhead.)

WINONA. I am Winona Tarlow.
JOHN. I am John Harper.
WORDY. I am Wordy Stratman.
ETHELYN. I am Ethelyn MacCormick.
CALEB. I am Caleb Stratman.
TESS. I am Tess Harper.

BILL. I am Bill Hoddupp.
EMIL. I am Emil the Fifth.
MAUDALINE. I am Maudaline Stratman.
CARL. I am Carl Pritchard.
ALICE. I am Alice Darke.
MOLLY. I am Molly Pritchard.
RAY. I am Ray MacCormick.

(Pause. WINONA looks up. Whooooosh. Halley's Comet STREAKS across the sky. Everyone looks up.)

WINONA. There is magic in the air tonight.

THE END

PROPS PRESET LIST

SR ACT I

I-1	Wedding band	John
	Earrings	
	Watch	
	Phrasebook	Ray

I-3	Coleman cooler	Emil
	Beer	John
	3 hay bales	John
		Bill
	Blanket	Ray
	1 lawn chair	Ray
	2 lawn chairs	Carl
	2 pies	Ethelyn
	Pie cutter	Ethelyn
	Pie plates	Ethelyn
	4 sparklers	Bill
	Matches/lighter	

I-4　Letter to Carl Pritchard on desk

I-5	Bank desk
	3 bank chairs
	Phone
	Lollipops
	Lollipop container
	Caleb's letter
	Caleb's loan file
	Desk calendar

I-7	Head of lettuce	Emil
I-8	Walkman	Ray

I-11	Hay bale Truck	Ray
	Thermos	Ethelyn
	Picnic basket	Ethelyn
	Food	Ethelyn
	Flashlight	Ethelyn

I-12	Piece of luggage	Vanna
	Foreclosure notice	In luggage

I-13	Cigarettes	Molly
	Matches/lighter	Molly

SL ACT I

I-1	FFA Manual	Wordy

I-3	2 game horseshoes	Wordy
	Small cooler	Alice
	Beers in cooler	Alice
	Satchel briefcase	Carl
	Folder with copies of perpetual debt information	In briefcase
	Suntan lotion	Ginny
	Sign up sheet	Alice
	2 pencils	Alice

I-4	Letter to Alice	On desk

I-5	FMHA desk	
	3 chairs	Ray, Alice
	Small desk plant	On desk
	Waste basket	On desk
	Phone	On desk
	Rolodex	On desk
	Adding machine/calculator	On desk
	MacCormick loan file	On desk
	Other papers	On desk
	Pens/pencils	On desk
	Styrofoam cup	On desk
	Ashtray	On desk
	Accordion file	Ethelyn
	Accounting ledger	Ethelyn
I-9	Daiquiri glass	Tess
	Daiquiri pitcher	Tess
I-11	Box of things	Tess
	Bundle of letters	In box
	Snap shots	In box
	Old pair ballet shoes	In box
	Diary	In box
	Easter egg	In box
	Sunglasses	In box
	Compact	In box
	Lip stuff	In box
	FMHA desk	
	Desk dressing	
	1 chair	Alice
	Waste basket	

	Bucket	Alice
	Wet towel(s)	In bucket
I-13	Head of lettuce	Ethelyn
	Walking stick	Ethelyn

UPC ACT I BELOW

I-1	Soda	Director
	Carry out bag	Cameraman
	Sandwiches/burgers	In bag
	Ketchup envelopes	In bag
	1 chair	Cameraman
	Notepad	Director
	Pencil	Director
	Headset	Cameraman
I-3	BBQ table	
	Tablecloth	On table
	Paper plates	On table
	Plate of ribs	On table
	Tongs for ribs	On table
	Pot of beans	On table
	Spoon for beans	On table
	2 hot dogs on plate	On table
	2 hamburgers on plate	On table
	Bowl of potato salad	On table
	Spoon for potato salad	On table
	Rolls and buns	On table
	Condiments	On table
	Green Jello	On table
	Glass bowl for Jello	On table

	Paper cups	On table
	Plastic utensils	On table
	Paper napkins	On table
	Pitcher of beverage	On table
I-5	1 stool	Bar
	3 plastic tumblers	Bar
	Soda	Bar
	Beer glass	Bar
	Beer	In glass
	1 slice pumpkin bread	Bar
	Plate	
	Chalk board	Door
	Beer clock	Door
	Chip rack	Door
	Bowl of beans/peas	Bar
	Pot to put B/P in	Bar
	Cafe table	
	2 cafe chairs	
	2 ashtrays	Bar & table
	Crisco can	Molly
	Kitchen canister of sugar	Molly
	2 measuring cups	Molly
	Spatula	Molly
	Wooden spoon	Molly
	Mixing bowl	Molly
I-9	2 henna caps	Winona & Tess
	2 towels	Winona & Tess
	1 kitchen chair	Tess
	Crochet hook	Tess

	Daiquiri in glass	Winona
	Cigarettes/lighter	Winona
I-11	Comforter	Tess
	2 pillows	Tess
I-12	Working microphone	Gameshow host
	1 crown	Tess
	1 sash	Tess
I-14	Bible	Bill
I-15	Chair	Cameraman
	Headset	Cameraman
	Carry out bag	Cameraman
	Ketchup envelopes	Cameraman
	Notepad	Director
	Pencil	Director
	Sandwiches/hamburgers	In bag
	Molly's school picture	Carl
I-16	Snow (oats)	For 6

UPC ACT I ABOVE

I-3 Flag

I-4 8 foreclosure notices

I-9 Table
Adding machine
John's papers

Pencils
Chair

| I-11 | 3 juggling balls | Molly |
| | 3 bales of hay | Molly/Wordy |

I-13	Foreclosure notice	Tess
	Wedding band	Tess
	Pair of earrings	Tess
	Watch	Tess

SR ACT II

| II-2 | Cordless phone | Ethelyn |
| | Torn piece of newspaper | Ethelyn |

| II-4 | Car keys (purse) | Ethelyn |

II-5	Hotline table	
	Papers	On table
	Doughnut box	On table
	Log sheets	On table
	Thermos	On table
	Styrofoam cups	On table
	Pencils	On table
	2 phones	On table
	2 chairs	Bill & Alice

| II-6 | Court order | John |

| II-7 | Hotline table | |
| | Papers | On table |

Doughnut box	On table
Log sheets	On table
Thermos	On table
Styrofoam cups	On table
Pencils	On table
2 phones	On table
2 chairs	

II-11	1 flashlight	Ethelyn

SL ACT II

II-2	Chair	Ethelyn
	Lamp w/cord	Ethelyn
II-4	Walkman	Ray
II-6	2 flashlights	Wordy, Caleb
	Shotgun	Caleb
II-8	2 stools	Wordy, Emil
	Change	Emil
II-9	Suitcase	Molly
	Photo of Molly as Clown	Molly
	Clown nose	Molly
II-11	1 flashlight	Ray
	Walkman	Ray
	2 shotguns	Ray

UPC ACT II BELOW

II-1	2 bar stools	
	Ashtray	
	3 coffee cups	
	Pot of coffee	
II-3	Henna cap	Winona
	Thermos of daiquiris	Winona
	Box of cornmeal	Winona
	Bouquet of flowers	John
II-8	Whiskey bottle	Emil
	2 shot glasses	Emil & Wordy
	Ashtray	Emil
II-9	Phone	Carl
	Key rack	Door
	Brochures	Door
	Basketball uniform	In box
	Box	
II-10	Auction lists	Auctioneers
	Thanksgiving table	
	Tablecloth	On table
	8 plates	On table
	8 place settings	On table
	8 glasses	On table
	8 napkins	On table
	Turkey	On platter
	Turkey platter	On table
	Basket of rolls	On table

Bowl of yams	On table
Bowl of cranberry jelly	On table
Bowl of green beans	On table
Bowl of dressing	On table
4 serving spoons	On table
Carving knife	Ethelyn's plate
Knife sharpener	Ethelyn's plate
2 candles	On table
Centerpiece	On table
4 wooden chairs	
4 kitchen chairs	
Bills and change	John
Photographs	Winona

UPC ACT II ABOVE

II-5 Table
      Phone
      Ashtray   Emil
      Chair
      Photos   Carl
      Hat   Carl
      Black drape

II-7 Table
      Phone   Caleb
      Chair
      Black drape

II-10 3 bales of hay   Auctioneer
      Megaphone   Auctioneer
      Clipboard   Auctioneer

About the Author

Heather McDonald was awarded a prestigious Playwrights' Center/McKnight Foundation Fellowship for 1987-1988. Her play *Faulkner's Bicycle* has been produced at Yale Repertory Theatre, off-Broadway at the Joyce Theatre-American Theatre Exchange, at American Playwrights Theatre, and in London on the fringe at the Bridge Lane Theatre. Another play, *Available Light,* was produced at the Actors Theatre of Louisville's Humana Festival of New Plays and off-off-Broadway by C&H Works. *The Rivers and Ravines* was commissioned and produced by the Arena Stage in 1988 and subsequently nominated for a Helen Hayes Award as Outstanding New Play. Ms. McDonald was a 1988 recipient of a Washington D.C. Commission on the Arts and Humanities grant.

OTHER TITLES AVAILABLE FROM SAMUEL FRENCH

TAKE HER, SHE'S MINE
Phoebe and Henry Ephron

Comedy / 11m, 6f / Various Sets
Art Carney and Phyllis Thaxter played the Broadway roles of
parents of two typical American girls enroute to college. The
story is based on the wild and wooly experiences the authors
had with their daughters, Nora Ephron and Delia Ephron,
themselves now well known writers. The phases of a girl's life
are cause for enjoyment except to fearful fathers. Through the
first two years, the authors tell us, college girls are frightfully
sophisticated about all departments of human life. Then they
pass into the "liberal" period of causes and humanitarianism,
and some into the intellectual lethargy of beatniksville. Finally,
they start to think seriously of their lives as grown ups. It's an
experience in growing up, as much for the parents as for the
girls.

"A warming comedy. A delightful play about parents vs kids.
It's loaded with laughs. It's going to be a smash hit."
– *New York Mirror*

MURDER AMONG FRIENDS
Bob Barry

Comedy Thriller / 4m, 2f / Interior

Take an aging, exceedingly vain actor; his very rich wife; a double dealing, double loving agent, plunk them down in an elegant New York duplex and add dialogue crackling with wit and laughs, and you have the basic elements for an evening of pure, sophisticated entertainment. Angela, the wife and Ted, the agent, are lovers and plan to murder Palmer, the actor, during a contrived robbery on New Year's Eve. But actor and agent are also lovers and have an identical plan to do in the wife. A murder occurs, but not one of the planned ones.

"Clever, amusing, and very surprising."
– *New York Times*

"A slick, sophisticated show that is modern and very funny."
– WABC TV

SAMUEL FRENCH STAFF

Nate Collins
President

Ken Dingledine
Director of Operations,
Vice President

Bruce Lazarus
Executive Director,
General Counsel

Rita Maté
Director of Finance

ACCOUNTING
Lori Thimsen | Director of Licensing Compliance
Nehal Kumar | Senior Accounting Associate
Glenn Halcomb | Royalty Administration
Jessica Zheng | Accounts Receivable
Andy Lian | Accounts Payable
Charlie Sou | Accounting Associate
Joann Mannello | Orders Administrator

BUSINESS AFFAIRS
Caitlin Bartow | Assistant to the Executive Director

CORPORATE COMMUNICATIONS
Abbie Van Nostrand | Director of Corporate
Communications

CUSTOMER SERVICE AND LICENSING
Brad Lohrenz | Director of Licensing Development
Laura Lindson | Licensing Services Manager
Kim Rogers | Theatrical Specialist
Matthew Akers | Theatrical Specialist
Ashley Byrne | Theatrical Specialist
Jennifer Carter | Theatrical Specialist
Annette Storckman | Theatrical Specialist
Dyan Flores | Theatrical Specialist
Sarah Weber | Theatrical Specialist
Nicholas Dawson | Theatrical Specialist
David Kimple | Theatrical Specialist

EDITORIAL
Amy Rose Marsh | Literary Manager
Ben Coleman | Literary Associate

MARKETING
Ryan Pointer | Marketing Manager
Courtney Kochuba | Marketing Associate
Chris Kam | Marketing Associate

PUBLICATIONS AND PRODUCT DEVELOPMENT
Joe Ferreira | Product Development Manager
David Geer | Publications Manager
Charlyn Brea | Publications Associate
Tyler Mullen | Publications Associate
Derek P. Hassler | Musical Products Coordinator
Zachary Orts | Musical Materials Coordinator

OPERATIONS
Casey McLain | Operations Supervisor
Elizabeth Minski | Office Coordinator, Reception
Coryn Carson | Office Coordinator, Reception

SAMUEL FRENCH BOOKSHOP (LOS ANGELES)
Joyce Mehess | Bookstore Manager
Cory DeLair | Bookstore Buyer
Sonya Wallace | Bookstore Associate
Tim Coultas | Bookstore Associate
Alfred Contreras | Shipping & Receiving

LONDON OFFICE
Anne-Marie Ashman | Accounts Assistant
Felicity Barks | Rights & Contracts Associate
Steve Blacker | Bookshop Associate
David Bray | Customer Services Associate
Robert Cooke | Assistant Buyer
Stephanie Dawson | Amateur Licensing Associate
Simon Ellison | Retail Sales Manager
Robert Hamilton | Amateur Licensing Associate
Peter Langdon | Marketing Manager
Louise Mappley | Amateur Licensing Associate
James Nicolau | Despatch Associate
Martin Phillips | Librarian
Panos Panayi | Company Accountant
Zubayed Rahman | Despatch Associate
Steve Sanderson | Royalty Administration Supervisor
Douglas Schatz | Acting Executive Director
Roger Sheppard | I.T. Manager
Debbie Simmons | Licensing Sales Team Leader
Peter Smith | Amateur Licensing Associate
Garry Spratley | Customer Service Manager
David Webster | UK Operations Director
Sarah Wolf | Rights Director

SAMUELFRENCH.COM
SAMUELFRENCH-LONDON.CO.UK

GET THE NAME OF YOUR CAST AND CREW IN PRINT WITH SPECIAL EDITIONS!

Special Editions are a unique, fun way to commemorate your production and RAISE MONEY.

The Samuel French Special Edition is a customized script personalized to *your* production. Your cast and crew list, photos from your production and special thanks will all appear in a Samuel French Acting Edition alongside the original text of the play.

These Special Editions are powerful fundraising tools that can be sold in your lobby or throughout your community in advance.

These books have autograph pages that make them perfect for year book memories, or gifts for relatives unable to attend the show. Family and friends will cherish this one of a kind souvenir.

Everyone will want a copy of these beautiful, personalized scripts!

ORDER YOUR COPIES TODAY!
E-MAIL SPECIALEDITIONS@SAMUELFRENCH.COM
OR CALL US AT 1-866-598-8449!